OPENING THE DOOR OF YOUR HEART

And other Buddhist tales of HAPPINESS

Ajahn Brahm was born in London in 1951. He regarded himself as a Buddhist at the age of sixteen after reading Buddhist books while still at school. His interest in Buddhism and meditation flourished while studying Theoretical Physics at Cambridge University. After completing his degree and teaching for a year, he travelled to Thailand to become a monk.

He was ordained in Bangkok at the age of twenty-three by the Abbot of Wat Saket. He subsequently spent nine years studying and training in the forest meditation tradition under Venerable Ajahn Chah.

In 1983, he was asked to assist in the establishment of a forest monastery near Perth, Western Australia. Ajahn Brahm is now the Abbot of Bodhinyana Monastery and the Spiritual Director of the Buddhist Society of Western Australia.

To my teacher, Ajahn Chah, who lived at peace,
To my fellow monks who remind me of the beauty of silence,
And to my father who taught me kindness.

Grant yourself a moment of peace,
and you will understand
how foolishly you have scurried about.

Learn to be silent,
and you will notice that
you have talked too much.

Be kind,
and you will realise that
your judgement of others was too severe.

— Ancient Chinese Proverb

OPENING THE DOOR OF YOUR HEART

And other Buddhist tales
of HAPPINESS

Ajahn Brahm

Buddhist Publication Society
Kandy Sri lanka

I wish to acknowledge Ron Storey for painstakingly typing up the first manuscript; my fellow monks for their guidance and help; and, lastly, my managing editor at Lothian Books, Magnolia Flora, for her advice and encouragement in this my first book.

Buddhist Publication Society
P.O. Box 61 • 54, Sangharaja Mawatha
Kandy, Sri Lanka
http://www.bps.lk • http://www.bpsbooks.com

First published 2004
BPS edition - 2006
Reprinted - 2007, 2011, 2013, 2014, 2017

National Library of Sri Lanka — Cataloguing-in-Publication data:

Brahmavamso Himi, Ajahn.
Opening the door of your heart and other Buddhist tales of happiness/Ajan Brahmawanso Himi. — Kandy: Buddhist Publication Society, 2006. — 206p.; 22 cm

ISBN 955-24-0285-9 Price:

i. 294.34435 DDC21 ii. Title
1. Buddhist meditation 2. Buddhism

ISBN 955-24-0285-9

Typeset at BPS.

Printed by
Ajith Printers (Pvt) Ltd.
342, Old Kesbewa Road, Rattanapitiya,
Boralesgamuwa, Sri Lanka.
Tel: +94 (0) 112517269

Contents

Introduction

Life is a series of interwoven stories, not a set of concepts. Ideas are generalisations, always some distance from the truth. A story, with all its array of meanings and richness of detail, is recognisably much closer to real life. That is why we relate more easily to stories than to abstract theories. We love a good yarn.

The stories in this book have been collected over the thirty years that I have lived as a monk in the forest tradition of Theravada Buddhism. For many centuries, Theravada has been the main vehicle of spirituality for the peoples of Thailand, Burma, Sri Lanka, Cambodia and Laos. Now this form of Buddhism is growing in the West—and in the South as I live in Australia!

I am often asked what the difference is between the major strands of Buddhism—Theravada, Mahayana, Vajrayana, and Zen. The answer is that they are like the same type of cake but each has a different icing: on the outside they may look and taste different, but when you dig deeply into the tradition, you find the same taste—the taste of freedom. There was only one Buddhism in the beginning.

The Buddha taught in northeast India around 2600 years ago—that's a century before Socrates. He taught not only monks and nuns, but also many thousands of ordinary people: from rice farmers to street sweepers and even prostitutes. The wisdom of the Buddha did not come as a revelation from a supernatural being. It arose from the deepest of insights into the true nature of life. The Buddha's teachings came from his heart, opened by deep meditation. As the Buddha famously said, 'It is in this fathom long body endowed with mind that the beginning and the end of this world are made known.'[1]

The Buddha's central teaching was the Four Noble Truths. Rearranging them from their usual order, these are:

1 Happiness
2 The cause of happiness
3 The absence of happiness
4 The cause for such an absence.

The stories in this book revolve around the Second Noble Truth, the cause of happiness.

The Buddha would often teach using stories. My teacher, the late Ajahn Chah of northeast Thailand, also taught using stories. After one of Ajahn Chah's discourses, it was the stories I would remember most, especially the funny ones. Moreover, it was these stories that conveyed the deepest instructions about the path to inner happiness. The story was the messenger carrying his teachings.

I have also used stories when teaching Buddhism and meditation in Australia, Singapore and Malaysia for more than twenty years, and I have presented some of the best of these stories in this book. The stories are intended to speak for themselves, so I have added minimal commentary. Each one carries many levels of meaning, so the more you read them, the more truths are revealed.

May you enjoy these stories of true happiness as much as those who have heard them told. And may they help change your life for the better, just as they have for so many others.

Ajahn Brahm
Perth, May 2004

Perfection and guilt

Two bad bricks

After we purchased the land for our monastery in 1983 we were broke. We were in debt. There were no buildings on the land, not even a shed. Those first few weeks we slept on old doors we had bought cheaply from the salvage yard; we raised them on bricks at each corner to lift them off the ground. (There were no mattresses, of course—we were forest monks.)

The abbot had the best door, the flat one. My door was ribbed with a sizeable hole in the centre where the door handle would have been. I was glad the doorknob had been removed, but that left a hole in the very centre of my door-bed. I joked that now I wouldn't need to get out of bed to go to the toilet! The cold truth was, however, that the wind would come up through the hole. I didn't sleep much those nights.

We were poor monks who needed buildings. We couldn't afford to employ a builder—the materials were expensive enough. So I had to learn how to build: how to prepare the foundations, lay concrete and bricks, erect the roof, put in the plumbing—the whole lot. I had been a theoretical physicist and high-school teacher in lay life, not used to working with my hands. After a few years, I became quite skilled at building, even calling my crew the BBC (Buddhist Building Company). But when I started it was very difficult.

It may look easy to lay a brick: just a dollop of mortar underneath, a little tap here, a little tap there. When I began laying bricks, I'd tap one corner down to make it level and another corner would go up. So I'd tap that corner down then the brick would move out of line. After I'd nudged it back into line, the first corner would be too high again. You try it!

Being a monk, I had patience and as much time as I needed. I made sure every single brick was perfect, no matter how long it took. Eventually, I completed my first brick wall and stood back to admire it. It was only then that I noticed—oh no!—I'd missed two bricks. All the other bricks were nicely in line, but these two were inclined at an angle. They looked terrible. They spoiled the whole wall. They ruined it.

By then, the cement mortar was too hard for the bricks to be taken out, so I asked the abbot if I could knock the wall down and start over again—or, even better, blow it up. I'd made a mess of it and I was very embarrassed. The abbot said no, the wall had to stay.

When I showed our first visitors around our fledgling monastery, I always tried to avoid taking them past my brick wall. I hated anyone seeing it. Then one day, some three or four months after I finished it, I was walking with a visitor and he saw the wall.

'That's a nice wall,' he casually remarked.

'Sir,' I replied in surprise, 'have you left your glasses in your car? Are you visually impaired? Can't you see those two bad bricks which spoil the whole wall?'

What he said next changed my whole view of that wall, of myself, and of many other aspects of life. He said, 'Yes. I can see those two bad bricks. But I can also see the 998 good bricks as well.'

I was stunned. For the first time in over three months, I could see other bricks in that wall apart from the two mistakes. Above, below, to the left and to the right of the bad bricks were good bricks, perfect bricks. Moreover, the perfect bricks were many, many more than the two bad bricks. Before, my eyes would focus exclusively on my two mistakes; I was blind to everything else. That was why I couldn't bear looking at that wall, or having others see it. That was why I wanted to destroy it. Now that I could see the good bricks, the wall didn't look so bad after all. It was, as the visitor had said, 'a nice brick wall'. It's still there now, twenty years later, but I've forgotten exactly where those bad bricks are. I literally cannot see those mistakes any more.

How many people end a relationship or get divorced because all they can see in their partner are 'two bad bricks'? How many of us become depressed or even contemplate suicide, because all we can see in ourselves are 'two bad bricks'. In truth, there are many, many more good bricks, perfect bricks—above, below, to the left and to the right of the faults—but at times we just can't see them. Instead, every time we look, our eyes focus exclusively on the mistakes. The mistakes are all we see, and they're all we think are there, so we want to destroy them. And sometimes, sadly, we do destroy a 'very nice wall'.

We've all got our two bad bricks, but the perfect bricks in each one of us are much, much more than the mistakes. Once we see this, things aren't so bad. Not only can we live at peace with ourselves, inclusive of our faults, but we can also enjoy living with a partner. This is bad news for divorce lawyers, but good news for you.

I have told this anecdote many times. After one occasion, a builder came up to me and told me a professional secret. 'We builders always make mistakes,' he said, 'But we tell our clients that it is "an original feature" with no other house in the neighbourhood like it. And then we charge them a couple of thousand dollars extra!'

So the 'unique features' in your house probably started out as mistakes. In the same way, what you might take to be mistakes in yourself, in your partner, or in life in general, can become 'unique features', enriching your time here, once you stop focusing on them exclusively.

The temple garden

Buddhist temples in Japan are renowned for their gardens. Many years ago, there was one temple that boasted the most beautiful garden of all. Travellers would come from all over the country just to admire its exquisite arrangement, so rich in simplicity.

An old monk came to visit once. He arrived very early, just after dawn. He wanted to discover why this garden was considered the most inspiring, so he concealed himself behind a large bush with a good view of the garden.

He saw a young gardening monk emerge from the temple carrying two wicker baskets. For the next three hours, he watched the young monk carefully pick up every leaf and twig that had fallen from the spreading plum tree in the centre of the garden. As he picked up each leaf and twig, the young monk would turn it over in his soft hand, examine it, ponder over it; and if it was to his liking he would delicately place it in one of the baskets. If it wasn't to be of use to him, he would drop it in the second basket, the rubbish basket. Having collected and thought over every leaf and twig, having emptied the rubbish basket on the pile at the rear of the temple, he paused to take tea and compose his mind for the next crucial stage.

The young monk spent another three hours, mindfully, carefully, skilfully, placing each leaf and twig just in the right place in the garden. If he wasn't satisfied with the position of a twig, he would turn it slightly or move it forwards a little until, with a light smile of satisfaction, he would move on to the next leaf, choosing just the right shape and colour for its place in the garden. His attention to detail was unparalleled. His mastery over the arrangement of colour and shape was superb. His understanding of natural beauty was sublime. When he was finished, the garden looked immaculate.

Then the old monk stepped out into the garden. From behind a broken-toothed smile, he congratulated the young gardening monk, 'Well done! Well done indeed, Venerable! I've been observing you all morning. Your diligence is worthy of the highest of praise. And your garden ... Well! Your garden is almost perfect.'

The young monk's face went white. His body stiffened as if he had been stung by a scorpion. His smile of self-satisfaction slipped from his face and tumbled into the great chasm of the void. In Japan, you can never be sure of old grinning monks!

'What d...do...you mean?' he stuttered through his fear. 'What do y...you mean, ALMOST perfect?' and he prostrated himself at the old monk's feet. 'Oh master! Oh teacher! Please release your compassion on me. You have surely been sent by the Buddha to show me how to make my garden really perfect. Teach me, Oh Wise One! Show me the way!'

'Do you really want me to show you?' asked the old monk, his ancient face creasing with mischief.

'Oh yes. Please do. Oh please master!'

So the old monk strode into the centre of the garden. He put his old but still strong arms around the leafy plum tree. Then with the laugh of a saint, he shook the hell out of that poor tree! Leaves, twigs and bark fell everywhere, and still the old monk shook that tree. When no more leaves would fall, he stopped.

The young monk was horrified. The garden was ruined. The whole morning's work was wasted. He wanted to kill the old monk. But the old monk merely looked around him admiring his work. Then with a smile that melts anger, he said gently to the young monk, 'Now your garden is really perfect.'

What's done is finished

The monsoon in Thailand is from July to October. During this period, the monks stop travelling, put aside all work projects and devote themselves to study and meditation. The period is called 'Vassa' or the 'Rains Retreat'.

In the south of Thailand some years ago, a famous abbot was building a new hall in his forest monastery. When the Rains Retreat came, he stopped all work and sent the builders home. This was the time for quiet in his monastery.

A few days later a visitor came, saw the half-constructed building and asked the abbot when his hall would be finished. Without hesitation, the old monk said, 'The hall is finished.'

'What do you mean, "The hall is finished"?' the visitor replied, taken aback. 'It hasn't got a roof. There are no doors or windows. There are pieces of wood and cement bags all over the place. Are you going to leave it like that? Are you mad? What do you mean, "The hall is finished"?'

The old abbot smiled and gently replied, 'What's done is finished,' and then he went away to meditate. That is the only way to have a retreat or to take a break. Otherwise our work is never finished.

The idiot's guide to peace of mind

I told the previous story to a large audience one Friday evening in Perth. On the following Sunday, an angry parent came to tell me off. He had attended that talk together with his teenage son. On Saturday evening, his son wanted to go out with his friends. The father asked him, 'Have you finished your homework yet, son?' His son replied,

'As Ajahn Brahm taught us at the temple last night, Dad, what's done is finished! See ya.'

The following week I told another story.

Most people in Australia have a garden with their house, but only a few know how to find peace in their garden. For the rest, the garden is just another place for work. So I encourage those with a garden to nurture its beauty by working a while, and nurture their hearts by just sitting peacefully in the garden, enjoying nature's gifts.

The first idiot thinks this a jolly good idea. So they decide to get all the little jobs out of the way first, and then they will allow themselves a few moments of peace in their garden. After all, the lawn does need mowing, the flowers could do with a good watering, the leaves need raking, the bushes need pruning, the path needs sweeping ... Of course, it takes up all of their free time just to get a fraction of those 'little jobs' out of the way. Their work is never finished, so they never get to have a few minutes of peace. Have you ever noticed that in our culture, the only people who 'rest in peace' are found in the cemetery?

The second idiot thinks they are much smarter than the first. They put away the rakes and the watering cans and sit out in the garden reading a magazine, probably with glossy pictures of nature. But that's enjoying your magazine, not finding peace in your garden.

The third idiot puts away all the gardening tools, all the magazines, newspapers and radios, and just sits in the peace of their garden ... for about two seconds! Then they start thinking: 'That lawn really needs mowing. And those bushes should be pruned soon. If I don't water those flowers within a few days they may die. And maybe a nice gardenia would go well in that corner. Yes! With one of those ornamental birdbaths in front. I could pick one up at the nursery ...' That is enjoying thinking and planning. There is no peace of mind there.

The smart gardener considers, 'I've worked long enough, now is the time to enjoy the fruit of my work, to listen for the peace. So even though the lawn needs mowing and the leaves need raking and blah! blah! blah! NOT NOW.' This way, we find the wisdom to enjoy the garden even though it's not perfect.

Perhaps there's an old Japanese monk hiding behind one of the bushes ready to jump out and tell us that our messy old garden really is perfect. Indeed, if we look at the work we have already done instead of focusing on the work that remains to be done, we might understand that what's done has been finished. But if we focus exclusively on the faults, on the things that need to be fixed, as in the case of my brick wall in my monastery, we will never know peace.

The intelligent gardener enjoys their fifteen minutes of peace in the perfect imperfection of nature, not thinking, not planning and not feeling guilty. We all deserve to get away and have some peace; and others deserve the peace of us getting out of their way! Then, after getting our crucial, life-saving fifteen minutes of peace 'out of its way', we carry on with our gardening duties.

When we understand how to find such peace in our garden, we will know how to find peace anytime, anywhere. Especially, we will know how to find peace in the garden of our heart, even though at times we might think that it's such a mess, with so much to be done.

Guilt and absolution

A few years ago, a young Australian woman came to see me at my temple in Perth. Monks are often sought out for advice on people's problems, perhaps because we're cheap—we never charge a fee. She was tormented with guilt. Some six months previously, she had been working in a remote mining community in the north of Western Australia. The work was hard and the money good, but there was not much to do in the hours off work. So one Sunday afternoon she suggested to her best friend, and her best friend's boyfriend, that they all go out for a drive in the bush. Her girlfriend didn't want to go, and neither did the boy, but it was no fun going alone. So she cajoled, argued and badgered until they gave in and agreed to go on the drive in the bush.

There was an accident: the car rolled on the loose gravel road. The young woman's girlfriend was killed; the boy was paralysed. The drive was her idea, yet she wasn't hurt. She told me with sorrow in her eyes: 'If only I hadn't forced them to go. She would still be here. He would still have his legs. I shouldn't have made them go. I feel so terrible. I feel so guilty.'

The first thought that came into my mind was to reassure her that it wasn't her fault. She didn't plan to have the accident. She had no intention of hurting her friends. These things happen. Let it go. Don't feel guilty. But the second thought that came up was, 'I bet she's heard that line before, hundreds of times, and it obviously hasn't worked.' So I paused, looked deeper into her situation, then told her it was good that she felt so guilty.

Her face changed from sorrow to surprise, and from surprise to relief. She hadn't heard this before: that she should feel guilty. I'd guessed right. She was feeling guilty about feeling guilty. She felt guilty and everyone was telling her not to. She felt 'double guilt', guilt over the accident and guilt over feeling guilty. Our complicated minds work like that.

Only when we had dealt with the first layer of guilt and established that it was all right for her to feel guilty could we proceed to the next stage of the solution: What's to be done about it?

There's a helpful Buddhist saying: 'Rather light a candle than complain about darkness.'

There's always something we can do instead of feeling upset, even if that something is just sitting peacefully for a while, not complaining.

Guilt is substantially different from remorse. In our culture 'guilty' is a verdict hammered out on hard wood by a judge in a court. And if no one else punishes us, we will look to punish ourselves, some way or another. Guilt means punishment deep in our psyche.

So the young woman needed a penance to absolve her from guilt. Telling her to forget it and get on with life wouldn't have worked. I suggested that she volunteer for work at her local hospital's rehab unit, treating the casualties of road accidents. For there, I thought, she would wear away her guilt with all the hard work, and also, as usually happens in voluntary work, be helped so much by the very people she was there to help.

Criminal guilt

Before I had the honourable but burdensome office of abbot dumped on me, I used to visit the prisons around Perth. I kept a careful record of the hours of service I had spent in jail to be used as credit in case I ever got sentenced!

On my first visit to a big prison in Perth, I was surprised and impressed at the number of prisoners who came to hear me speak on meditation. The room was packed. Around ninety-five per cent of the prisoner population had come to learn meditation. The longer I spoke, the more restless my captive audience grew. After only ten minutes, one of the prisoners, one of the leading crims in the jail, put up his hand to interrupt my talk and ask a question. I invited him to go ahead and ask.

'Is it really true,' he said, 'that through meditation you can learn how to levitate?'

Now I knew why so many prisoners had come for my talk. They were all planning to learn meditation so they could levitate over the walls! I told them that it is possible, but only for exceptional meditators, and then only after many years of training. The next time I went to teach at that prison, only four prisoners turned up for the session.

Over the many years that I taught inside prisons, I got to know some of the crims very well indeed. One thing I discovered was that every crim feels guilty for what they have done. They feel it day and night, deep in their hearts. They only tell this to their close friends. They wear the standard defiant prisoner face for viewing in public. But when you earn their trust, when they take you as their spiritual guide for a while, then they open themselves and reveal their painful guilt. I would often help them with the next story: the story of the Class B kids.

The Class B kids

Many years ago, an experiment in education was carried out in secrecy at a school in England. The school had two classes for the same age of children. At the end of the school year an examination was held, in order to select the children for the classes of next year. However, the results of the exam were never revealed. In secrecy, with only the principal and the psychologists knowing the truth, the child who came first in the exam was placed in the same class with the children who came fourth and fifth, eighth and ninth, twelfth and thirteenth, and so on.

While the children who came second and third in the exam were placed in the other class, with the children who came sixth and seventh, tenth and eleventh, and so on. In other words, based on their performance in the exam, the children were split evenly between the two classes. Teachers for the next year were carefully selected for equal ability. Even the classrooms were chosen with similar facilities. Everything was made as equal as possible, except for one thing: one was called 'Class A', the other was called 'Class B'.

In fact, the classes had children of equal ability. But in everyone's mind the children in Class A were the clever ones, and the kids of Class B were not so clever. Some of the parents of the Class A children were pleasantly surprised that their child had done so well and rewarded them with favours and praise, whereas the parents of some of the Class B kids berated their children for not working hard enough and took away some of their privileges. Even the teachers taught the Class B kids in a different manner, not expecting so much from them. For a whole year the illusion was maintained. Then there was another end-of-year exam.

The results were chilling, but not surprising. The children of Class A performed so much better than those of Class B. In fact, the results were just as if they had been the top half chosen from last year's exam. They had become Class A children. And those in the other group, though equal the year before, had now become Class B kids. That was what they were told for a whole year, that was how they were treated, and that was what they believed—so that was what they became.

The child in the supermarket

I tell my 'jailbird buddies' never to think of themselves as criminals, but as someone who has done a criminal act. Because if they are told they are criminals, if they are treated as criminals and if they believe they are criminals, they become criminals. That's how it works.

A young boy dropped a carton of milk at the supermarket checkout and it split open, spilling milk all over the floor. 'You stupid child!' said the mother.

In the very next aisle, another boy dropped a carton of honey. It broke open too, spreading honey over the floor. 'That was a stupid thing you did,' said his mother.

The first child has been classified stupid for life; the other has had only one fault pointed out. The first will probably become stupid; the other will learn to stop doing stupid things.

I ask my jailbird buddies what else they did the day of their crime? What else did they do the other days of that year? What else did they do the other years of their life? Then I repeat the story of my brick wall. There are other bricks in the wall that represent our life apart from our crimes. In fact, the good bricks are always many, many more than the bad. Now, are you a bad wall deserving destruction? Or are you a good wall with a couple of bad bricks, just like the rest of us?

A few months after I became abbot and stopped visiting jails, I received a personal phone call from one of the prison officers. He asked me to come back. He gave me a compliment I will always treasure. He told me that my jailbird buddies, my students, once they had finished their sentences, never returned to jail.

We are all criminals

In the previous story I talked about people I worked with in jail, but the message applies to anyone 'doing time' in the prison of guilt. That 'crime' for which we feel guilty—what else did we do that day, that year, this life? Can we see the other bricks in the wall? Can we see beyond the stupid act causing our guilt? If we focus on the 'Class B' act too long, we might become a 'Class B' person: that's why we keep repeating our mistakes and amassing more guilt. But when we see the other parts of our lives, the other bricks in our wall, when we gain a realistic perspective, then a wonderful insight opens like a flower in the heart: we deserve to be forgiven.

Letting go of guilt, forever

The most difficult stage of the journey out of guilt is convincing ourselves that we deserve to be forgiven. The stories given so far are there to assist us, but the final step out of the prison is made alone.

When he was still a young boy, a friend of mine was playing with his best friend on a pier. For a joke, he pushed his friend into the water. The friend drowned. For many years that young man lived with crippling guilt. The drowned friend's parents lived next door. He grew up knowing that he had deprived them of their son. Then one morning, as he told it to me, he realised he didn't need to feel guilty any more. He walked out of his own prison into the warm air of freedom.

Love and commitment

Unconditional love

When I was around the age of thirteen, my father took me aside and told me something that would change my life. The two of us were alone in his beaten-up old car, in a side street of one of the poorer suburbs of London. He turned to me and said this: 'Son, whatever you do in your life, know this. The door of my house will always be open to you.'

I was only a young teenager at the time. I didn't really understand what he meant, but I knew it was something important, so I remembered it. My father would be dead three years later.

When I became a monk in northeast Thailand, I thought over those words of my Dad. Our home at that time was a small council flat in a poor part of London, not much of a house to open a door into. But then I realised this was not what my Dad really meant. What was lying within my father's words, like a jewel wrapped in a cloth, was the most articulate expression of love that I know: 'Son, whatever you do in your life, know this. The door of my *heart* will always be open to you.'

My father was offering unconditional love. No strings attached. I was his son and that was enough. It was beautiful. It was real. He meant it.

It takes courage and wisdom to say those words to another, to open the door of your heart to somebody else, with no 'ifs'. Perhaps we might think they would take advantage of us, but that's not how it works, not in my experience. When you are given that sort of love from another, it's like receiving the most precious of gifts. You treasure it, keep it close to your heart, lest it be lost. Even though at the time I only partially understood my Dad's meaning, even so I wouldn't dare hurt such a man. If you give those words to someone close to you, if you really mean them, if they come from your heart, then that person will reach upwards, not downwards, to meet your love.

Opening the door of your heart

Several centuries ago, seven monks were in a cave in a jungle somewhere in Asia, meditating on the type of unconditional love I described in the previous story. There was the head monk, his brother and his best friend. The fourth was the head monk's enemy: they just could not get along. The fifth monk in the group was a very old monk, so advanced in years that he was expected to die at any time. The sixth monk was sick—so ill in fact that he too could die at any time. And the last monk, the seventh, was the useless monk. He always snored when he was supposed to be meditating; he couldn't remember his chanting, and if he did he would chant off-key. He couldn't even keep his robes on properly. But the others tolerated him and thanked him for teaching them patience.

One day a gang of bandits discovered the cave. It was so remote, so well hidden, that they wanted to take it over as their own base, so they decided to kill all the monks. The head monk, fortunately, was a very persuasive speaker. He managed—don't ask me how—to persuade the gang of bandits to let all the monks go, except one, who would be killed as a warning to the other monks not to let anyone know the location of the cave. That was the best the head monk could do.

The head monk was left alone for a few minutes to make the awful decision of who should be sacrificed so that the others could go free.

When I tell this story in public, I pause here to ask my audience, 'Well, who do you think the head monk chose?' It stops some of my audience from going to sleep during my talk, and it wakes up the others who are already asleep. I remind them that there was the head monk, the brother, the best friend, the enemy, the old monk and the sick monk (both close to death), and the useless monk. Who do you think he chose?

Some then suggest the enemy. 'No,' I say.

'His brother?'

'Wrong.'

The useless monk always gets a mention—how uncharitable we are! Once I have had my bit of fun, I reveal the answer: the head monk was unable to choose.

His love for his brother was exactly the same, no more and no less, than his love for his best friend—which was exactly the same as his love for his enemy, for the old monk, the sick monk, and even for the dear old useless monk. He had perfected the meaning of those words: the door of my heart will always be open to you, whatever you do, whoever you are.

The door of the head monk's heart was wide open to all, with unconditional, non-discriminating, free-flowing love. And most poignantly, his love for others was equal to his love for himself. The door of his heart was open to himself as well. That's why he couldn't choose between himself and others.

I remind the Judaeo-Christians in my audience that their books say to 'love thy neighbour as thy self'. Not more than yourself and not less than yourself, but equal to yourself. It means to regard others as one would regard oneself, and oneself as one regards others.

Why is it that most in my audience thought that the head monk would choose himself to die? Why is it, in our culture, that we are always sacrificing ourselves for others and this is held to be good? Why is it that we are more demanding, critical and punishing of ourselves than of anyone else? It is for one and the same reason: we have not yet learned how to love ourselves. If you find it difficult to say to another 'the door of my heart is open to you, whatever you do', then that difficulty is trifling compared with the difficulty you will face in saying to yourself, 'Me. The one I've been so close to for as long as I can remember. Myself. The door of my heart is open to me as well. All of me no matter what I have done. Come in.'

That's what I mean by loving ourselves: it's called forgiveness. It is stepping free from the prison of guilt; it is being at peace with oneself. And if you do find the courage to say those words to yourself, honestly, in the privacy of your inner world, then you will rise up, not down, to meet sublime love. One day, we all have to say to ourselves those words, or ones similar, with honesty, not playing games. When we do, it is as if a part of ourselves that had been rejected, living outside in the cold for so long, has now come home. We feel unified, whole, and free to be happy. Only when we love ourselves in such a way can we know what it means to really love another, no more and no less.

And please remember you do not have to be perfect, without fault, to give yourself such love. If you wait for perfection, it never arrives. We must open the door of our heart to ourselves, *whatever we have done*. Once inside, then we are perfect.

People often ask me what happened to those seven monks when the head monk told the bandits that he was unable to choose.

The story, as I heard it many years ago, didn't say: it stopped where I have finished.[2] But I know what happened next; I figured out what must have ensued. When the head monk explained to the bandits why he couldn't choose between himself and another, and described the meaning of love and forgiveness as I have just done for you, then all the bandits were so impressed and inspired that not only did they let the monks live, but they became monks themselves!

Marriage

Since I became a celibate monk, I have married many women.

Part of my job as a Buddhist monk is to perform the religious part of Buddhist marriage ceremonies. According to my tradition of Buddhism, a lay Buddhist is the official marriage celebrant, but many of the couples regard me as the one who married them. So I have married many women and many men as well.

It is said that there are three rings to a marriage: the engagement ring, the wedding ring, and the suffer-ring!

So trouble is to be expected. When there is trouble, the people I have married often come to talk to me. Being a monk who likes an easy life, I include in my marriage service the next three stories, intended to keep the three of us out of trouble for as long as possible.

Commitment

My view of relationships and marriage is this: when the couple are going out, they are merely involved; when they become engaged, they are still only involved, maybe more deeply; when they publicly exchange marriage vows, that is commitment.

The meaning of the marriage ceremony is the commitment. During a ceremony, to drive home the meaning in a way people usually remember for the rest of their lives, I explain that the difference between involvement and commitment is the same as the difference between bacon and eggs.

At this point, the in-laws and friends start to pay attention. They begin to wonder, 'What has bacon and eggs got to do with marriage?' I continue.

'With bacon and eggs, the chicken is only involved, but the pig is committed. Let this be a pig marriage.'

The chicken and the duck

This was a favourite story of my teacher, Ajahn Chah of northeast Thailand.

A newly married couple went for a walk together in a wood, one fine summer's evening after dinner. They were having such a wonderful time being together until they heard a sound in the distance: 'Quack! Quack!'

'Listen,' said the wife, 'That must be a chicken.'

'No, no. That was a duck,' said the husband.

'No, I'm sure that was a chicken,' she said.

'Impossible. Chickens go "Cock-a-doodle-doo", ducks go "Quack! Quack!" That's a duck, darling,' he said, with the first signs of irritation.

'Quack! Quack!' it went again.

'See! It's a duck,' he said.

'No dear. That's a chicken. I'm positive,' she asserted, digging in her heels.

'Listen wife! That … is … a … duck. D-U-C-K, duck! Got it?' he said angrily.

'But it's a chicken,' she protested.

'It's a blooming duck, you, you …'

And it went 'Quack! Quack!' again before he said something he oughtn't.

The wife was almost in tears. 'But it's a chicken.'

The husband saw the tears welling up in his wife's eyes and, at last, remembered why he had married her. His face softened and he said gently, 'Sorry, darling. I think you must be right. That is a chicken.'

'Thank you, darling,' she said and she squeezed his hand.

'Quack! Quack!' came the sound through the woods, as they continued their walk together in love.

The point of the story that the husband finally awakened to was, who cares whether it is a chicken or a duck? What was much more important was their harmony together, that they could enjoy their walk on such a fine summer's evening. How many marriages are broken over unimportant matters? How many divorces cite 'chicken or duck' stuff?

When we understand this story, we will remember our priorities. The marriage is more important than being right about whether it is a chicken or a duck. Anyway, how many times have we been absolutely, certainly and positively convinced we are right, only to find out we were wrong later? Who knows? That could have been a genetically modified chicken made to sound like a duck!

(For the sake of gender equality and a peaceful life as a monk, each time I tell the story I usually switch around the one who says it's a chicken and the one who says it's a duck.)

Gratitude

After a wedding ceremony in Singapore a few years ago, the father of the bride took his new son-in-law aside to give him some advice on how to keep the marriage long and happy. 'You probably love my daughter a lot,' he said to the young man.

'Oh yes!' the young man sighed.

'And you probably think that she is the most wonderful person in the world,' the old man continued.

'She's so perfect in each and every way,' the young man cooed.

'That's how it is when you get married,' said the old man. 'But after a few years, you will begin to see the flaws in my daughter. When you do begin to notice her faults, I want you to remember this. If she didn't have those faults to begin with, son-in-law, she would have married someone much better than you!'

So we should always be grateful for the faults in our partner because if they didn't have those faults from the start, they would have been able to marry someone much better than us.

Romance

When we are in love, we see only the 'good bricks' in our partner's wall. That is all we want to see, so that is all we do see. We are in denial. Later, when we go to our lawyer to file for divorce, we only see the bad bricks in our partner's wall. We are blind to any redeeming qualities. We don't want to see those, so we don't see them. We go into denial again.

Why is it that romance happens in a darkly lit nightclub, or at an intimate dinner by candlelight, or at night under the moonlight? It is because, in those situations, you can't see all her pimples, or his false teeth. But under candlelight, our imagination is free to fantasise that the girl sitting opposite could be a supermodel, or the man has the looks of a movie star. We love to fantasise, and we fantasise to love. At least we should know what we're doing.

Monks aren't into candle-lit romance. They're into turning up the lights on reality. If you want to dream, don't visit a monastery. In my first year as a monk in northeast Thailand, I was travelling in the back of a car with two other Western monks, and with Ajahn Chah, my teacher, sitting in the front passenger seat. Ajahn Chah suddenly turned around and looked at the young American novice monk sitting next to me, and then said something in Thai. The third Western monk in the car was fluent in Thai and translated for us: 'Ajahn Chah says that you are thinking about your girlfriend back in L.A.'

The jaw of the American novice dropped almost to the floor. Ajahn Chah had been reading his thoughts—accurately. Ajahn Chah smiled, and his next words were translated as, 'Don't worry. We can fix that. Next time you write to her, ask her to send to you something personal, something intimately connected to her, which you can bring out whenever you miss her, to remind you of her.'

'Is that allowable for a monk?' asked the novice, surprised.

'Sure,' said Ajahn Chah.

Perhaps monks understand romance after all.

What Ajahn Chah said next took many minutes to translate. Our translator had to stop laughing and pull himself together first.

'Ajahn Chah says ...' He struggled to get the words out, wiping away tears of mirth. 'Ajahn Chah says you should ask her to send you a bottle of her shit. Then whenever you miss her, you can bring out the bottle and open it!'

Well, it is something personal. And when we express our love for our partner, don't we say we love everything about them? The same advice would be given to a nun missing her boyfriend.

As I said, if you want the fantasy of romance, steer clear of our monastery.

True love

The trouble with romance is that when the fantasy is broken, the disappointment can badly hurt us. In romantic love, we don't really love our partner, we only love the way they make us feel. It is the 'high' we feel in their presence that we love. Which is why, when they are absent, we miss them and ask to be sent a bottle of … (see the previous story). Like any 'high', it wears out after a while.

True love is selfless love. We are concerned only for the other person. We tell them, 'The door of my heart will always be open to you, whatever you do', and we mean it. We just want them to be happy. True love is rare.

Many of us like to think that our special relationship is true love, not romantic love. Here is a test for you to discover which type of love it is.

Think of your partner. Picture them in your mind. Recall the day you came together and the wonderful times you have enjoyed ever since. Now imagine receiving a letter from your partner. It tells you that they have fallen deeply in love with your best friend, and the two of them have run away to live together. How would you feel?

If it were true love, you would be so thrilled that your partner has found someone even better than you, and is now even more happy. You would be delighted that your partner and best friend were having such a good time together. You'd be ecstatic that they were in love. Isn't your partner's happiness the most important thing in true love?

True love is rare.

A Queen was looking through the palace window at the Buddha walking for alms food in the city. The King saw her and grew jealous of her devotion to the Great Monk. He confronted his Queen and demanded to know who she loved most, the Buddha or her husband? She was a devoted disciple of the Buddha, but in those days you had to be very careful if your husband was the King. Losing your head meant losing your head. She kept her head and replied with searing honesty, 'I love myself more than the both of you.'[3]

Fear and pain

Freedom from fear

If guilt is looking at the brick wall of our past and seeing only the two bad bricks we've laid, then fear is staring at the brick wall of our future and seeing only what might go wrong. When we are blinded by fear, we just can't see the rest of the wall that's made up of what might go perfectly well. Fear, then, is overcome by seeing the whole of the wall, as in the following story from a recent teaching visit to Singapore.

My series of four public talks had been arranged many months before, the large and expensive 2500-seat auditorium at Singapore's Suntec City had been booked, and the posters were displayed on the bus stops. Then came the crisis of SARS (Severe Acute Respiratory Syndrome). When I arrived in Singapore the schools were all closed, apartment blocks were quarantined and the government was advising its people not to attend any public gatherings. Fear was vast at that time. I was asked, 'Should we cancel?'

That very morning, the front page of the daily newspaper warned in large black figures that ninety-nine Singaporeans were now confirmed with SARS. I asked what the current population of Singapore was. It was approximately four million. 'So,' I remarked, 'that means that 3,999,901 Singaporeans haven't got SARS! Let's go ahead!' 'But what if someone gets SARS?' fear said.

'But what if they don't?' said wisdom. And wisdom had probability on its side.

So the talks went ahead. Fifteen hundred people came on the first night, and the numbers steadily increased to a full house on the final night. Around 8000 people attended those talks. They learned to go against irrational fear, and that would strengthen their courage in the future. They enjoyed the talks and left happy, which meant that their virus-fighting immune system had been enhanced. And, as I emphasised at the end of each talk, because they laughed at my funny stories, they have exercised their lungs and thus strengthened their respiratory systems! Of course, not one person from those audiences got SARS.

The possibilities for the future are infinite. When we focus on the unfortunate possibilities, that's called fear. When we remember the other possibilities, which are usually more likely, that's called freedom from fear.

Predicting the future

Many people would like to know the future. Some are too impatient to wait for it to happen, so they seek out the services of oracles and fortune-tellers. I have a warning for you on oracles: never trust a poor fortune-teller!

Meditating monks are regarded as excellent fortune-tellers, but they usually don't co-operate easily.

One day a long-serving disciple of Ajahn Chah asked the great master to predict his future. Ajahn Chah refused: good monks don't tell fortunes. But the disciple was determined. He reminded Ajahn Chah of how many times he had offered him alms food, how many donations he had given to his monastery, and how he had chauffeured Ajahn Chah in his own car at his own expense, to the neglect of his own work and family. Ajahn Chah saw that the man was determined to get his fortune told, so he said that for once he would make an exception to the no-fortune-telling rule. 'Give me your hand. Let me see your palm.'

The disciple was excited. Ajahn Chah had never read palms for any other disciple. This was special. Moreover, Ajahn Chah was regarded as a saint, with great psychic powers. Whatever

Ajahn Chah said would happen, surely would happen. Ajahn Chah traced the lines on the disciple's palm with his own index finger. Every so often, he would say to himself, 'Ooh. That's interesting' or 'Well, well, well' or 'Amazing'. The poor disciple was in a frenzy of anticipation.

When Ajahn Chah was finished, he let go of the disciple's hand and said to him, 'Disciple, this is how your future will turn out.'

'Yes, yes,' said the disciple quickly.

'And I am never wrong,' added Ajahn Chah.

'I know, I know. Well. What's my future going to be?' the disciple uttered in ultimate excitement.

'Your future will be uncertain,' said Ajahn Chah. And he wasn't wrong!

Gambling

Money is hard to accumulate, but easy to lose—and the easiest way to lose it is by gambling. All gamblers are losers, eventually. Still, people like to predict the future so that they can make a lot of money by gambling. I tell the following two stories to show them how dangerous it is to predict the future, even when we have signs.

A friend awoke one morning from one of those dreams that was so vivid it seemed real. He had dreamt that five angels had given him five big jars of gold worth a fortune. When he opened his eyes, there were no angels in his bedroom and, alas, no pots of gold. But it was a very strange dream.

When he went into the kitchen, he saw that his wife had made him five boiled eggs with five pieces of toast for his breakfast. At the top of the morning newspaper he noticed the date, the fifth of May (the fifth month). Something odd was going on. He turned to the back pages of the newspaper, to the horse racing pages. He was stunned to see that at Ascot (five letters), in race number five, horse number five was called … Five Angels! The dream was an omen.

He took the afternoon off work. He drew five thousand dollars out of his bank account. He went to the race track, to the fifth bookmaker and made his bet: five thousand dollars on horse number five, race number five, Five Angels, to win. The dream couldn't be wrong. The lucky number five couldn't be wrong! The dream wasn't wrong. The horse came in fifth.

The second story occurred in Singapore a few years ago. An Australian man married a nice Chinese woman from Singapore. Once, while they were visiting family in Singapore, his brothers-in-law were going to the horse racing track for the afternoon and invited him to go along too. He agreed. But before they visited the racetrack, they insisted on stopping off at a renowned Buddhist temple to light some joss sticks and pray for good luck. When they arrived at the small temple, they found it was in a mess. So they got some brooms, a mop and some water and cleaned it all up. Then they lit their joss sticks, asked for good luck, and went off to the track. They all lost heavily.

That night, the Australian had a dream of a horse race. When he awoke, he clearly remembered the name of the winning horse. When he saw in the *Straits Times* that there was, indeed, a horse by that name running in a race that afternoon, he rang his brothers-in-law to tell them the good news. They refused to believe that a Chinese spirit guarding a Singaporean temple would tell a white man the name of a winning horse, so they disregarded his dream. He went to the track. He put a large bet on that horse. The horse won.

Chinese temple spirits must like Australians. His brothers-in-law were fuming.

What is fear?

Fear is finding fault with the future. If only we could keep in mind how uncertain our future is, then we would never try to predict what could go wrong. Fear ends right there.

Once, when I was little, I was terrified of going to the dentist. I had an appointment and did not want to go. I worried myself silly. When I arrived at the dentist's, I was told my appointment had been cancelled. I learned what a waste of precious time fear is.

Fear is dissolved in the uncertainty of the future. But if we don't use our wisdom, fear can dissolve us. It nearly dissolved the young novice Buddhist monk, Little Grasshopper, in an old television series called *Kung Fu*. I used to watch this series obsessively in my last year as a schoolteacher, before I became a monk.

One day, Little Grasshopper's blind master took the novice into a back room of the temple, normally kept locked. In the room was an indoor pool some six metres wide, with a narrow wooden plank as a bridge from one side to the other. The master warned Little Grasshopper to keep clear of the pool's edge, because it did not contain water, but very strong acid.

'In seven days' time,' Grasshopper was told, 'you will be tested. You will have to walk across that pool of acid by balancing on the wooden plank. But be careful! Do you see at the bottom of that pool of acid those bones here and there?'

Grasshopper looked warily over the edge and saw the many bones.

'They used to belong to young novices like you.'

The master took Grasshopper out of that terrible room into the sunlight of the temple courtyard. There, the elder monks had set up a plank of exactly the same size as the one over the acid pool, but raised on two bricks. For the next seven days, Grasshopper had no other duties apart from practising walking on that plank.

It was easy. In a few days he could walk with perfect balance, blindfolded even, across that plank in the courtyard. Then came the test.

Grasshopper was led by his master into the room with the acid pool. The bones of the novices who had fallen in shimmered at the bottom. Grasshopper got up onto the end of the plank and looked round at his master. 'Walk,' he was told.

A plank over acid is much narrower than a plank of the same size in a temple courtyard. Grasshopper began to walk, but his step was unsteady; he began to sway. He wasn't even halfway across. He wobbled even more. It looked like he was going to fall into the acid. Then the series stopped for a commercial break.

I had to endure those stupid advertisements, all the while worrying how poor Little Grasshopper would save his bones.

The ads ended, and we were back in the acid-pool room, with Grasshopper beginning to lose his confidence. I saw him step unsteadily. Then sway. Then he fell in!

The old blind master laughed, hearing Little Grasshopper splash about in the pool. It wasn't acid; it was only water. The old bones had been tossed in as 'special effects'. They had fooled Little Grasshopper, as they had fooled me.

'What made you fall in?' asked the master seriously. 'Fear made you fall in, Little Grasshopper, only fear.'

Fear of public speaking

I was told that one of the greatest fears people have is speaking in public. I have to speak a lot in public, in temples and at conferences, at marriages and funerals, on talkback radio and even on live television. It is part of my job.

I remember one occasion, five minutes before I was to give a public talk, when fear overwhelmed me. I hadn't prepared anything; I had no idea what I was going to say. About three hundred people were sitting in the hall expecting to be inspired. They had given up their evening to hear me talk. I began thinking to myself: 'What if I can't think of anything to say? What if I say the wrong thing? What if I make a fool of myself?'

All fear begins with the thought 'what if' and continues with something disastrous. I was predicting the future, and with negativity. I was being stupid. I knew I was being stupid; I knew all the theory, but it wasn't working. Fear kept rolling in. I was in trouble.

That evening I developed a trick, what we call in monk-speak 'a skilful means', which overcame my fear then, and which has worked ever since. I decided that it didn't matter if my audience enjoyed the talk or not, as long as I enjoyed my talk. I decided to have fun.

Now, whenever I give a talk, I have fun. I enjoy myself. I tell funny stories, often at my own expense, and laugh at them with the audience. On live radio in Singapore I told Ajahn Chah's prediction about the currency of the future. (Singaporeans are interested in things economic.)

Ajahn Chah predicted once that the world would run out of paper for bank notes and metal for coins, so the people would have to find something else for everyday transactions. He predicted that they would use little pellets of chicken shit for money. People would go around with their pockets full of chicken shit. Banks would be full of the stuff and robbers would try to steal it. Rich people would be so proud of how much chicken shit they owned and poor people would dream of winning a big pile of chicken shit in the lottery. Governments would focus excessively on the chicken shit situation in their country, and environmental and social issues would be considered later, once there was enough chicken shit to go around.

What is the essential difference between banknotes, coins and chicken shit? None.

I enjoyed telling that story. It makes a poignant statement about our current culture. And it is fun. The Singaporean listeners loved it.

I figured out once that if you decide to have fun when you give a public talk, then you relax. It is psychologically impossible to have fear and fun at the same time. When I am relaxed, ideas flow freely into my mind during my talk, then leave through my mouth with the smoothness of eloquence. Moreover, the audience doesn't get bored when it is fun.

A Tibetan monk once explained the importance of making the audience laugh during a talk.

'Once they open their mouths,' he said, 'then you can throw in the pill of wisdom!'

I never prepare my talks. I prepare my heart and mind instead. Monks in Thailand are trained never to prepare a talk, but to be prepared to talk without notice at any time.

It was *Magha Puja,* the second most important Buddhist festival of the year in northeast Thailand. I was at Ajahn Chah's monastery, Wat Nong Pah Pong, with some two hundred monks and many thousands of lay people. Ajahn Chah was very famous; it was my fifth year as a monk.

After the evening service, it was time for the main talk. Ajahn Chah would usually give the talk at such a major occasion, but not always. Sometimes he would look down the line of monks and, if his eyes stopped at yours, then you were in trouble. He would ask you to give the sermon. Even though I was such a young monk compared to many others ahead of me, one could never be sure of anything around Ajahn Chah.

Ajahn Chah looked down the line of monks. His eyes reached me and went past. I silently sighed with relief. Then his eyes came back up the line again. Guess where they stopped?

'Brahm,' Ajahn Chah ordered, 'give the main sermon.'

There was no way out. I had to give an unprepared talk in Thai for an hour, in front of my teacher, fellow monks and thousands of lay people. It didn't matter whether it was a good sermon or not. It mattered only that I did it.

Ajahn Chah never told you whether it was a good talk or not. That wasn't the point. Once he asked a very skilled Western monk to give a sermon to the laypeople who had assembled at his monastery for the weekly observance. At the end of an hour, the monk began to wrap up his sermon in Thai. Ajahn Chah interrupted him and told him to continue for another hour. That was tough. Still, he did it. As he prepared to finish up after struggling for the second hour in Thai, Ajahn Chah ordered another hour of sermon. It was impossible. Westerners only know so much Thai. You end up repeating yourself over and over. The audience gets bored. But there wasn't any choice. At the end of the third hour, most people had left anyway, and the ones remaining were talking among themselves. Even the mosquitoes and the wall lizards had gone to sleep. At the end of the third hour, Ajahn Chah ordered another hour! The Western monk obeyed. He said that after such an experience (and the talk did end after the fourth hour), when you have plumbed the very depths of audience response, you no longer fear speaking in public.

That was how we were trained by the great Ajahn Chah.

Fear of pain

Fear is the major ingredient of pain. It is what makes pain hurt. Take away the fear and only feeling is left.

In the mid-1970s, in a poor and remote forest monastery in northeast Thailand, I had a bad toothache. There was no dentist to go to, no telephone and no electricity. We didn't even have any aspirin or paracetamol in the medicine chest. Forest monks were expected to endure.

In the late evening, as often seems to happen with sickness, the toothache grew steadily worse and worse. I considered myself quite a tough monk but that toothache was testing my strength. One side of my mouth was solid with pain. It was by far the worst toothache I had ever had, or have ever had since. I tried to escape the pain by meditating on the breath. I had learned to focus on my breath when the mosquitoes were biting; sometimes I counted forty on my body at the same time, and I could overcome one feeling by focusing on another. But this pain was extraordinary. I would fill my mind with the feeling of the breath for only two or three seconds, then the pain would kick in the door of the mind that I'd closed, and come bursting in with a furious force.

I got up, went outside and tried walking meditation. I soon gave that up too. I wasn't 'walking' meditation; I was 'running' meditation. I just couldn't walk slowly. The pain was in control: it made me run. But there was nowhere to run to. I was in agony. I was going crazy.

I ran back into my hut, sat down and started chanting. Buddhist chants are said to possess supernormal power. They can bring you fortune, drive away dangerous animals, and cure sickness and pain—or so it is said. I didn't believe it. I'd been trained as a scientist. Magic chanting was all hocus-pocus, only for the gullible. So I began chanting, hoping beyond reason that it would work. I was desperate. I soon had to stop that too. I realised I was shouting the words, screaming them. It was very late and I was afraid I would wake up the other monks. With the way I was bellowing out those verses, I would probably have woken the whole village a couple of kilometres away! The power of the pain wouldn't let me chant normally.

I was alone, thousands of miles from my home country, in a remote jungle with no facilities, in unendurable pain with no escape. I'd tried everything I knew, everything. I just couldn't go on. That's what it was like.

A moment of sheer desperation like that unlocks doors into wisdom, doors that are never seen in ordinary life. One such door opened to me then, and I went through it. Frankly, there was no alternative.

I remembered two short words: 'let go'. I had heard those words many times before. I had expounded on their meaning to my friends. I thought I knew what they meant: such is delusion. I was willing to attempt anything, so I tried letting go, one-hundred per cent letting go. For the first time in my life, I really let go.

What happened next shook me. That terrible pain immediately vanished. It was replaced with the most delectable bliss. Wave upon wave of pleasure thrilled through my body. My mind settled into a deep state of peace, so still, so delicious. I meditated easily, effortlessly now. After my meditation, in the early hours of the morning, I lay down to get some rest. I slept soundly, peacefully. When I woke up in time for my monastic duties, I noticed I had a toothache. But it was nothing compared to the previous night.

Letting go of pain

In the previous story, it was the fear of the pain of that toothache that I had let go of. I had welcomed the pain, embraced it and allowed it to be. That was why it went.

Many of my friends who have been in great pain have tried out this method and found it does not work! They come to me to complain, saying my toothache was nothing compared to their pain. That's not true. Pain is personal and cannot be measured. I explain to them why letting go didn't work for them using this story of my three disciples.

The first disciple, in great pain, tries letting go.

'Let go,' they suggest, gently, and wait.

'Let go!' they repeat when nothing changes.

'Just let go!'

'Come on, Let Go.'

'I'm telling you, Let! Go!'

'LET GO!'

We may find this funny, but that is what we all do most of the time. We let go of the wrong thing. We should be letting go of the one saying, 'Let go.' We should be letting go of the 'control freak' within us, and we all know who that is. Letting go means 'no controller'.

The second disciple, in terrible pain, remembers this advice and lets go of the controller. They sit with the pain, assuming that they're letting go. After ten minutes the pain is still the same, so they complain that letting go doesn't work. I explain to them that letting go is not a method for getting rid of pain, it is a method for being free from pain. The second disciple had tried to do a deal with pain: 'I'll let go for ten minutes and you, pain, will disappear. OK?'

That is not letting go of pain; that is trying to get rid of pain.

The third disciple, in horrible pain, says to that pain something like this: 'Pain, the door to my heart is open to you, whatever you do to me. Come in.'

The third disciple is fully willing to allow that pain to continue as long as it wants, even for the rest of their life; to allow it even to get worse. They give the pain freedom. They give up trying to control it. That is letting go. Whether the pain stays or goes is now all the same to them. Only then does the pain disappear.

TM or how to transcend-dental medication

A member of our community has very bad teeth. He has needed to have many teeth pulled out, but he'd rather not have the anaesthetic. Eventually, he found a dental surgeon in Perth who would extract his teeth without anaesthetic. He has been there several times. He finds it no problem.

Allowing a tooth to be extracted by a dentist without anaesthetic might seem impressive enough, but this character went one better. He pulled out his own tooth without anaesthetic.

We saw him, outside the monastery workshop, holding a freshly pulled tooth smeared with his blood, in the claws of an ordinary pair of pliers. It was no problem: he cleaned the pliers of blood before he returned them to the workshop.

I asked him how he had managed to do such a thing. What he said exemplifies why fear is the major ingredient of pain. 'When I decided to pull out my own tooth—it was such a hassle going all the way to the dentist—it didn't hurt. When I walked to the workshop, that didn't hurt. When I picked up the pair of pliers, it didn't hurt. When I held the tooth in the grip of the pliers, it still didn't hurt. When I wiggled the pliers and pulled, it hurt then, but only for a couple of seconds. Once the tooth was out, it didn't hurt much at all. It was only five seconds of pain, that's all.'

You, my reader, probably grimaced when you read this true story. Because of fear, you probably felt more pain than he did! If you tried the same feat, it would probably hurt terribly, even before you reached the workshop to get the pliers. Anticipation—fear—is the major ingredient of pain.

No worries

Letting go of 'the controller', staying more with this moment and being open to the uncertainty of our future, releases us from the prison of fear. It allows us to respond to life's challenges with our own original wisdom, and gets us out safely from many a sticky situation.

I was standing in one of the six queues at the immigration barrier at Perth airport, returning from a wonderful trip to Sri Lanka via Singapore. The queues were moving slowly; they were obviously doing a thorough check. A customs officer emerged from a side door in the lobby, leading a small sniffer-dog trained to detect drugs. The incoming travellers smiled nervously as the customs officer led the sniffer dog up and down each line. Even though they were not carrying any drugs, you could detect a release of tension after the dog sniffed them and moved away to someone else.

When the cute little dog reached me and sniffed, it stopped. It buried its little muzzle in my robe at the waist and wagged its tail in rapid, wide arcs. The customs officer had to yank at the leash to pull the dog away. The passenger in line ahead of me, who had been quite friendly before, had now moved a step further away from me. And I was sure that the couple behind had moved a step backwards.

After five minutes, I was much closer to the counter, when they brought the sniffer dog around again. Up and down the lines the dog went, giving each traveller a little sniff and then moving on. When it came to me it stopped again. Its head went in my robe and its tail went crazy. Again, the customs officer had to forcefully pull the dog away. I felt all eyes on me now. Even though many people might become a little worried at this point, I was completely relaxed. If I went to jail, well, I had many friends there and they feed you much better than they do in a monastery!

When I reached the customs check, they gave me a thorough search. I had no drugs: monks don't even take alcohol. They didn't strip-search me; I think this was because I showed no fear. All they did was ask me why I thought the sniffer-dog had stopped only at me. I said that monks have great compassion for animals, and maybe that was what the dog sniffed; or maybe the dog was a monk in one of its past lives. They let me go through after that.

I came very close to getting punched once, by a big Australian who was angry and half-drunk. Lack of fear saved the day as well as my nose.

We had just moved into our new city temple, a little to the north of Perth. We were having a grand opening ceremony and, to our surprise and delight, the then Governor of Western Australia, Sir Gordon Reid, and his wife, had accepted our invitation to attend. I was given the job of organising the marquee for the courtyard and the chairs for the visitors and VIPs. I was told by our treasurer to get the very best; we wanted to put on a very good show.

After a little searching, I found a very expensive hire company. It was located in one of the rich western suburbs of Perth and hired out marquees for the garden parties of the millionaires. I explained what I wanted and why it had to be the best. The woman with whom I dealt said she understood, so the order was placed.

When the marquee and chairs arrived late on Friday afternoon, I was around the back of our new temple helping someone else. When I came to check the delivery, the truck and the men had already gone. I couldn't believe the state of the marquee. It was covered with red dust. I was disappointed, but the problem could be fixed. We began to hose the marquee down. Then I checked the visitors chairs and they were just as filthy. Rags were brought out and my priceless volunteers began to clean each chair. Lastly, I looked at the special chairs for the VIPs. They were special: not one had legs the same length! They all wobbled, a lot.

This was unbelievable. This was too much. I rushed to the phone, called the hire company and caught the woman just as she was about to leave for the weekend. I explained the situation, emphasising that we can't have the Governor of WA rocking on a wobbly chair during the ceremony. What if he falls off? She understood, apologised, and assured me that she would have the chairs changed within the hour.

This time I waited for the delivery truck. I saw it turning into our road. Halfway up the road, some sixty metres from the temple, with the truck still travelling quite fast, one of the men jumped out and came running toward me with wild eyes and a clenched fist.

'Where's the bloke in charge?' he yelled. 'I want to see the bloke in charge!'

I was to find out later that our first delivery was their last for the week. After us, the men had tidied up and retired to the pub to begin the weekend. They must have been well into their weekend drinking when the manager came into the pub and ordered them all back to work. The Buddhists needed their chairs changed.

I went up to that man and said gently, 'I'm the bloke in charge. How can I help?'

He moved his face closer to mine, with his right fist still clenched, almost touching my nose. His eyes were burning with anger. I smelt the strong odour of beer from his mouth only a few inches away. I felt neither fear nor arrogance. I just relaxed.

My so-called friends stopped cleaning the chairs to watch. Not one of them came to help me. Thanks a lot, friends! The face-off lasted a couple of minutes. I was fascinated by what was happening. That angry worker was frozen by my response. His conditioning was only used to seeing fear or counter-aggression. His brain did not know how to respond to someone relaxed when one of his fists was next to their nostrils. I knew he could not punch me, nor move away. Fearlessness bewildered him.

In those few minutes the truck had parked and the boss came towards us. He put his hand on the frozen worker's shoulder and said, 'Come on, let's unload the chairs.' That broke the impasse, giving him a way out.

I said 'Yes. I'll give you a hand.' And we unloaded the chairs together.

Anger and forgiveness

Anger

Anger is not a clever response. Wise people are happy, and happy people don't get angry. Firstly, anger is irrational.

One day when our monastery vehicle pulled up at a red traffic light alongside another car I noticed that the driver of the other vehicle was ranting at the lights: 'You damn traffic lights! You knew I had an important appointment. You knew I was running late. And you let that other car through just ahead of me, you swine! And this is not the first time either …'

He was blaming the traffic lights, as if they had much choice. He thought the traffic lights hurt him on purpose: 'Ah-hah! Here he comes. I know he's late. I'll just let this other car through first and then … Red! Stop! Got 'im!' The traffic lights might appear malicious, but they're just being traffic lights, that's all. What do you expect from traffic lights?

I imagined him reaching home late and his wife ranting at him, 'You damn husband! You knew we had an important appointment. You knew not to be late. And you saw to other business ahead of me, you swine! And this is not the first time either …'

She was blaming her husband, as if he had much choice. She thought her husband hurt her on purpose: 'Ah-hah! I've got an appointment with my wife. I'll be late. I'll just see to this other person first. Late! Got 'er.' Husbands might appear malicious, but they're just being husbands, that's all. What do you expect from husbands?

The characters in this story may be changed to suit most occasions of anger.

The trial

In order to express your anger, you have to justify it to yourself first. You have to convince yourself that anger is deserved, appropriate, right. In the mental process that is anger, it is as if a trial occurs in your mind.

The accused stands in the dock in the court in your mind. You are the prosecutor. You know they are guilty, but, to be fair, you have to prove it to the judge, your conscience, first. You launch into a graphic reconstruction of the 'crime' against you.

You infer all sorts of malice, duplicity and sheer cruelty of intention behind the accused's deed. You dredge up from the past their many other 'crimes' against you to convince your conscience that they deserve no mercy.

In a real court of law, the accused has a lawyer too who is allowed to speak. But in this mental trial, you are in the process of justifying your anger. You don't want to hear pathetic excuses or unbelievable explanations or weak pleas for forgiveness. The lawyer for the defence is not allowed to speak. In your one-sided argument, you construct a convincing case. That's good enough. Conscience brings down the hammer and they're GUILTY! Now we feel OK at being angry with them.

Many years ago, this is the process I saw happen in my own mind whenever I got angry. It seemed so unfair. So the next time I wanted to get angry with someone, I paused to let 'the defence lawyer' have their say. I thought up plausible excuses and probable explanations for their behaviour. I gave importance to the beauty of forgiveness. I found that conscience would not allow a verdict of guilty any more. It became impossible to judge the behaviour of another. Anger, not being justifiable, was starved of its food and died.

The retreat

The trigger for much of our anger is frustrated expectation. We sometimes invest so much of ourselves in a project that when it doesn't turn out as it *should* we become irritated. All 'shoulds' point to an expectation, a prediction for the future. We might have realised by now that the future is uncertain, unpredictable. Relying too much on an expectation for the future, a 'should', is asking for trouble.

A Western Buddhist I knew many years ago became a monk in the Far East. He joined a very strict, remote, meditation monastery, in the mountains. Every year they held a sixty-day meditation retreat. It was tough; it was rigid, not for weak minds.

They rose at 3.00 a.m. and by 3.10 a.m. they were sitting cross-legged in meditation. The whole day was regimented into a routine of fifty minutes sitting meditation, ten minutes walking meditation, fifty minutes sitting meditation, ten minutes walking meditation, and so on. They took their meals in the meditation hall, sitting cross-legged in their meditation place; no talking was allowed. At 10.00 p.m. they could lie down to sleep, but only in the meditation hall in the same spot where they had been meditating. Getting up at 3.00 a.m. was optional: you could get up earlier if you wanted, but not later! The only break was for the daily interview with the fearsome master, and short toilet breaks of course.

After three days, the legs and back of the Western monk were very sore. He was not used to sitting so long in a position that was so uncomfortable for a Westerner. Moreover, he still had another eight weeks to go. He began to doubt seriously whether he could endure such a long retreat.

At the end of the first week, things weren't getting any better. He was often in agony, sitting like that hour after hour.

Those who have been on a ten-day meditation retreat would know how painful it can get. He had another seven-and-a-half weeks to face.

This man was tough-minded. He gathered all his determination and endured, second by second. By the end of the first fortnight he'd really had enough: the pain was too much. His Western body wasn't cut out for this sort of treatment. This was not Buddhism, the Middle Way. Then he looked around at the Asian monks, also gritting their teeth, and pride pushed him through another fortnight. During this time, his body felt as if on fire with pain. His only relief was the 10.00 p.m. gong, when he could stretch out his tortured body to relax. But it seemed that as soon as he disappeared in sleep, the 3.00 a.m. gong would sound, waking him to another day of torment.

At the end of the thirtieth day, hope twinkled dimly in the distance. He was now past the halfway mark. He was on the home stretch, 'almost there,' he thought trying to convince himself. The days grew longer and the pain in his knees and back grew sharper. At times he thought he would cry. Still, he pushed through. Two weeks to go. One week to go. In that last week, time dragged like an ant stuck in treacle. Even though he was now used to enduring pain, it was no easier. To give in now, he thought, would be unfaithful to all he had endured so far. He was going to see it through, even if it killed him; and at times he thought it might.

He woke up to the 3.00 a.m. gong of the sixtieth day. He was almost there. The pain on that last day was incredible. As if pain had only been teasing him up to then, but now was pulling no punches. Even though there were only a few hours to go, he wondered if he would make it. Then came the final fifty minutes. He began that session imagining all the things he would do, starting in only one hour's time, when the retreat was over: the long hot bath, the leisurely meal, talking, lounging—then the pain interrupted his planning, demanding all of his mind. He opened his eyes slightly, secretly, several times during that last session to peek at the clock. He couldn't believe that time was strolling so slowly. Maybe the batteries in the clock needed changing? Maybe the clock would stop altogether with the hands forever stuck five minutes before the end of the retreat? The final fifty minutes were like fifty aeons, but even eternity must come to an end someday. And so it did. The gong sounded, so sweetly, for the end of the retreat.

Waves of pleasure coursed through his body, driving the pain deep into the background. He'd made it. Now he would treat himself. Bring on the bath!

The master rang the gong again to get everyone's attention. He had an announcement to make. He said, 'This had been an exceptional retreat. Many monks have made great progress and some have suggested to me, in their private interviews, that the retreat should be extended for another two weeks. I think this is a magnificent idea. The retreat is extended. Carry on sitting.'

All the monks folded their legs again and sat motionless in meditation, to begin another two weeks. The Western monk said that he didn't feel any pain in his body any more. He was just trying to figure out who those damn monks were who suggested the extension, and thinking what he was going to do to them once he found out! He hatched the most unmonkish plans for those uncaring monks. His anger blotted out all pain. He was incensed. He was murderous. He had never felt so much anger before. Then the gong sounded again. It was the quickest fifteen minutes of his life.

'Retreat over,' the master said. 'There are refreshments for you all in the refectory. Go at your leisure. You may talk now.'

The Western monk was lost in confusion. 'I thought we were meditating for another two weeks. What's going on?' A senior monk who spoke English saw his bewilderment and came over. Smiling, he said to the Westerner, 'Don't worry! The master does the same every year!'

The anger-eating demon

A problem with anger is that we enjoy being angry. There is an addictive and powerful pleasure associated with the expression of anger. And we don't want to let go of what we enjoy. However, there is also a danger in anger, a consequence that outweighs any pleasure. If we only realised the fruit of anger, and remembered the connection, then we would be willing to let anger go.

In a palace, in a realm a long time ago, a demon walked in while the King was away. The demon was so ugly, he smelled so bad and what he said was so disgusting that the guards and other palace workers froze in horror. This allowed the demon to stride right through the outer rooms, into the royal audience hall, and then sit himself on the King's throne. Seeing the demon on the King's throne, the guards and the others came to their senses.

'Get out of here!' they shouted. 'You don't belong there! If you don't move your butt right now, we'll carve it out with our swords!'

At these few angry words, the demon grew a few inches bigger, his face grew uglier, the smell got worse and his language became even more obscene.

Swords were brandished, daggers pulled out, threats made. At every angry word or angry deed, even at every angry thought, that demon grew an inch bigger, more ugly in appearance, more smelly and more foul in his language.

The confrontation had been going on for quite a while when the King returned. He saw on his own throne this gigantic demon. He had never seen anything so repulsively ugly before, not even in the movies. The stench coming from the demon would even make a maggot sick. And the language was more repugnant than anything you'd hear in the roughest of drunk-filled downtown bars on a Saturday night.

The King was wise. That's why he was King: he knew what to do.

'Welcome,' said the King warmly. 'Welcome to my palace. Has anyone got you anything to drink yet? or to eat?'

At those few kind gestures, the demon grew a few inches smaller, less ugly, less smelly and less offensive.

The palace personnel caught on very quickly. One asked the demon if he would like a cup of tea. 'We have Darjeeling, English Breakfast or Earl Grey. Or do you prefer a nice Peppermint? It's good for your health.' Another phoned out for pizza, family size for such a big demon, while others made sandwiches: devilled-ham of course. One soldier gave the demon a foot massage, while another massaged the scales on his neck. 'Mmmm! That was nice,' thought the demon.

At every kind word, deed or thought the demon grew smaller and less ugly, smelly and offensive. Before the pizza boy arrived with his delivery, the demon had already shrunk to the size he was when he first sat on the throne. But they never stopped being kind. Soon the demon was so small that he could hardly be seen. Then after one more act of kindness he vanished completely away.

We call such monsters 'anger-eating demons'.[4]

Your partner can sometimes be an 'anger-eating demon'. Get angry with them and they get worse—more ugly, more smelly and more offensive in their speech. The problem gets an inch bigger every time you are angry with them, even in thought. Perhaps you can see your mistake now and know what to do.

Pain is another 'anger-eating demon'. When we think with anger, 'Pain! Get out of here! You don't belong!', it grows an inch bigger and worse in other ways. It is difficult to be kind to something so ugly and offensive as pain, but there will be times in our life when we have no other option. As in the story of my toothache on pages 44–45, when we welcome pain, truly, sincerely, it becomes smaller, less of a problem, and sometimes vanishes completely.

Some cancers are 'anger-eating demons', ugly and repugnant monsters sitting in our body, our 'throne'. It is natural to say 'Get out of here! You don't belong!' When all else fails, or maybe even earlier, perhaps we can say, 'Welcome.' Some feed on stress—that's why they are 'anger-eating demons'. Those kinds of cancers respond well when the 'King of the Palace' courageously says: 'Cancer, the door of my heart is fully open to you, whatever you do. Come in!'

Right! That's it! I'm leaving!

Another of the consequences of anger that we should keep in mind is that it destroys our relationships and separates us from our friends. Why is it that having spent many happy years with a companion, when they make one mistake which hurts us badly, we get so angry that we end the relationship forever? All the wonderful moments we have shared together (the 998 good bricks) count as nothing. We only see that one dreadful mistake (the two bad bricks) and destroy the whole thing. It doesn't seem fair. If you want to be lonely, then cultivate anger.

A young Canadian married couple that I knew were finishing up a work contract in Perth. When planning their return to their hometown of Toronto, they had the ingenious idea of sailing to Canada. They planned to buy a small yacht and, with the help of another young married couple, sail it across the Pacific to Vancouver. There they would sell the yacht, recover their investment and have the deposit for their next home. Not only did it make sound financial sense, but it was also an adventure of a lifetime for the two young couples.

When they had arrived safely in Canada, they sent a letter to my monastery describing the wonderful journey. In particular, they related one incident that showed how stupid we can be when we are angry, and the reason anger must be resolved.

In the middle of their journey, somewhere in the Pacific, many, many kilometres from the nearest land, their yacht's engine broke down. The two men changed into work gear, went down into the small engine compartment and tried to repair the engine. The two women were sitting on the deck, enjoying the warm sun and reading magazines.

The engine compartment was hot and very cramped. To the men, it seemed as if the engine was being wilful and didn't want to be fixed. Big steel nuts wouldn't turn to the spanner, small but vital screws would slip and fall into the most inaccessible greasy recess, and leaks just wouldn't stop leaking. Frustration bred irritation, first with the engine, then with each other. Irritation grew quickly into anger. Then anger exploded into the madness of rage. One of the men had had enough. He threw down his wrench and shouted, 'Right! That's it! I'm leaving.'

Such is the madness of anger that he went to his cabin, cleaned up, changed clothes and packed his bags. He then appeared on deck, still fuming, in his best jacket with his bags in either hand. The two women said they nearly fell off the boat, they were laughing so much. The poor man looked around to see ocean, everywhere, as far as the horizon in every direction. There was nowhere to go.

The man felt such a fool; he reddened with embarrassment. He turned and went back to his cabin. He then unpacked, got changed, and returned to the engine compartment to give a hand. He had to. There was nowhere else to go.

How to stop an insurgency

When we realise that there is nowhere else to go, we face the problem rather than running away. Most problems have solutions that we can't see when we're running in the other direction. In the previous story, the engine of the yacht was fixed, the two men remained best friends, and they had a marvellous time on the rest of the voyage—together.

As the people of our world come to live ever closer to each other, we have to find solutions to our problems. There's no place to run away to. We simply cannot afford major conflicts any more.

In the mid to late 1970s I had personal experience of how a national government found such a solution to a major crisis, one that threatened the very existence of their democracy.

South Vietnam, Laos and Cambodia fell to the Communists within a few days of each other in 1975. The 'Domino Theory' current at that time among the Western powers, predicted that Thailand would soon fall next. I was a young monk in northeast Thailand during that period. The monastery in which I mostly lived was twice as close to Hanoi as it was to Bangkok. We were told to register with our embassies and evacuation plans were prepared. Most Western governments were to be surprised that Thailand didn't fall.

Ajahn Chah was quite famous by then and many top Thai generals and senior members of the national government would travel to his monastery for advice and inspiration. I had become fluent in Thai, and some Lao, and so gained an insider's understanding of the seriousness of the situation. The military and the government were not as concerned with the Red armies outside their borders as they were with the Communist activists and sympathisers within their own nation.

Many brilliant Thai university students had fled to the jungles in northeast Thailand to support an internal, Thai, Communist guerrilla force. Their weaponry was supplied from beyond Thailand's borders as was their training. But the villages in the 'pink' parts of the region gladly supplied their food and other requirements. They had local support. They were an ominous threat.

The Thai military and government found the solution in a three part strategy.

1 **Restraint**

The military did not attack the Communist bases, though every soldier knew where they were. When I was living the life of a wandering monk in 1979–80, seeking out the mountains and jungles to meditate in solitude, I would run into the army patrols and they would give me advice. They would point to one mountain and tell me not to go there—that was where the Communists were. Then they would point to another mountain and tell me that was a good place to meditate, there were no Communists there. I had to heed their advice. That year the Communists had caught some wandering monks meditating in the jungle and killed them—after torturing them, I was told.

2 **Forgiveness**

Throughout this dangerous period, there was an unconditional amnesty in place. Whenever one of the Communist insurgents wanted to abandon his cause, he could simply give up his weapon and return to his village or university. He would probably experience surveillance, but no punishments were imposed. I reached one village in Kow Wong district a few months after the Communists had ambushed and killed a large jeep full of Thai soldiers outside their village. The young men of the village were mostly sympathetic to the Communist soldiers, but not actively fighting. They told me they were threatened and harassed, but allowed to go free.

3 **Solving the root-problem**
During these years, I saw new roads being built and old roads being paved in the region. Villagers could now take their produce to town to sell. The King of Thailand personally supervised, and paid for, the construction of many hundreds of small reservoirs with connected irrigation schemes, allowing the poor farmers of the northeast to grow a second crop of rice each year. Electricity reached the remotest of hamlets and with it came a school and a clinic. The poorest region in Thailand was being cared for by the government in Bangkok, and the villagers were becoming relatively prosperous.

A Thai government soldier on patrol in the jungle told me once:

> We don't need to shoot the Communists. They are fellow Thais. When I meet them coming down from the mountains or going to the village for supplies, and we all know who they are, I just show them my new wristwatch, or let them listen to a Thai song on my new radio—then they give up being a Communist.

That was his experience, and that of his fellow soldiers.

The Thai Communists began their insurgency so angry with their government that they were ready to give their young lives. But restraint on the part of the government helped to prevent their anger being made worse. Forgiveness, through an amnesty, gave them a safe and honourable way out. Solving the problem, through development, made the poor villagers prosperous. The villagers saw no need to support the Communists anymore: they were content with the government they already had. And the Communists themselves began to doubt what they were doing, living with such hardships in the jungle-covered mountains.

One by one they gave up their guns and returned to their family, their village or their university. By the early 1980s, there were hardly any insurgents left, so then the generals of the jungle army, the leaders of the Communists, also gave themselves up. I remember seeing a feature article in the *Bangkok Post* of a sharp entrepreneur who was taking Thai tourists into the jungle to visit the now abandoned caves from where the Communists once threatened their nation.

What happened to those leaders of the insurgency? Could the same unconditional offer of amnesty be applied to them? Not quite. They were not punished, nor exiled. Instead, they were offered important positions of responsibility in the Thai government service, in recognition of their leadership qualities, capacity for hard work and concern for their people! What a brilliant gesture. Why waste the resource of such courageous and committed young men?

This is a true story as I heard if from the soldiers and villagers of northeast Thailand at the time. It is what I saw with my own eyes. Sadly, it has hardly been reported elsewhere.

At the time of writing this book, two of those former Communist leaders were serving their country as ministers in the Thai National Government.

Cooling off with forgiveness

When someone has hurt us, we don't have to be the one who punishes them. If we are a Christian, a Muslim or a Jew, surely we would believe that God will punish them enough? If we are a Buddhist, a Hindu or a Sikh, we would know that karma will provide our assailant with their just deserts. And if you are a follower of the modern religion of psychotherapy, you know that your assailant will have to go through years of expensive therapy because of their guilt! So why do we have to be the one who 'teaches them a lesson'? Considering wisely, we discover that we don't have to be the executioner. We are still doing our public duty when we let go of our anger and cool off with forgiveness.

Two of my fellow Western monks were having an argument. One of the monks was a former US marine who had fought as a 'grunt' (frontline soldier) in the Vietnam War and had been badly wounded. The other had been a very successful businessman who had made such a large amount of money that he had 'retired' in his mid-twenties. They were two clever, strong, extremely tough characters.

Monks aren't supposed to have arguments, but they were. Monks aren't supposed to have fist fights, but they were about to. They were eyeball to eyeball, nose to nose, and spitting anger. In the midst of a ferocious verbal exchange, the former marine got down on his knees and bowed gracefully to the shocked ex-businessman monk. Then he looked up and said, 'I'm sorry. Forgive me.'

It was one of those rare gestures that come direct from the heart, which are always spontaneous and inspirational rather than planned. They are recognisable by their immediacy, and their being totally irresistible.

The ex-businessman monk wept.

A few minutes later they were seen walking together as friends. Monks are supposed to do that.

Positive forgiveness

Forgiveness might work in a monastery, I hear you say, but if we give that sort of forgiveness in real life, we'll be taken advantage of. People will walk all over us—they'll just think we're weak. I agree. Such forgiveness rarely works. As the saying goes, 'He who turns the other cheek, must visit the dentist twice, rather than once!'

The Thai government, in the previous story, did more than just give forgiveness through its unconditional amnesty. It also sought out the root-problem, poverty, and tackled it skilfully. That was why the amnesty worked.

I call such forgiveness 'positive forgiveness'. 'Positive' means the positive reinforcement of those good qualities that we want to see appear. 'Forgiveness' means letting go of the bad qualities that are part of the problem—not dwelling on them, but moving on. For example, in a garden, watering only the weeds is like cultivating problems; not watering anything is like practising only forgiveness; and watering the flowers but not the weeds symbolises 'positive forgiveness'.

Some ten years ago, at the end of one of our Friday night talks in Perth, a woman came up to speak with me. She had been regularly attending these weekly talks for as long as I could remember, but this was the first time she had spoken to me. She said that she wanted to say a big thank you, not only to me, but also to all the monks who had taught at our centre. Then she explained why. She had begun coming to our temple seven years previously. She wasn't all that interested in Buddhism at that time, she confessed, nor in meditation. Her main reason for attending was as an excuse to get out of her house.

She had a violent husband. She was a victim of horrendous domestic violence. In those days, support structures just weren't available to help such a victim. In such a cauldron of boiling emotions, she couldn't see clearly enough to simply walk out forever. So she came to our Buddhist centre, with the idea that two hours in the temple was two hours she wouldn't be bashed.

What she heard in our temple changed her life. She listened to the monks describe positive forgiveness. She decided to try it out on her husband. She told me that every time he hit her, she forgave him and let it go. How she could do that, only she knows. Then every time he did, or said, anything kind, no matter how trifling, she would hug him or cover him with kisses or use any other gesture to let him know how much that kindness meant to her. She took nothing for granted.

She sighed and told me that it took her seven long years. At this point her eyes became watery, and so did mine. 'Seven long years,' she told me, 'and now you wouldn't recognise the man. He's changed completely. We have such a precious, loving relationship now, and two wonderful children.' Her face radiated the glow of a saint. I felt like getting on my knees to bow to her. 'See that stool?' she said, stopping me, 'He made that wooden meditation stool for me this week as a surprise. If it had been seven years ago, he would only have used it to hit me with!' The lump in my throat cleared as I laughed with her.

I admire that woman. She earned her own happiness, which was considerable, I would say, from the brightness of her features. And she changed a monster into a caring man. She helped another person, magnificently. That was an extreme example of positive forgiveness, recommended only for those heading for sainthood. Nevertheless, it shows what can be achieved when forgiveness is joined with encouraging the good.

Creating happiness

Flattery gets you everywhere

We all like to hear ourselves praised but unfortunately most of the time we only hear about our faults. That's fair, I suppose, because most of the time we only speak about someone else's faults. We hardly ever speak praise. Try listening to yourself speaking.

Without praise, without positive reinforcement of good qualities, those qualities wither and die. But a little bit of praise is a grandstand of encouragement. We all want to hear ourselves praised; we just want to be sure about what we have to do to hear it.

I once read in a magazine about a therapy group that used positive reinforcement for young children who had a rare eating disorder. Whenever these children ate solid food, they would vomit it up almost immediately. When any child managed to keep a morsel of food down for a minute or more, the group would throw a party. The parents would put on paper hats and stand on the chairs shouting and clapping; the nurses would dance and throw coloured streamers; someone would play the children's favourite music. There was suddenly a huge celebration, with the child who had kept their food down at the centre of it all.

The children began to keep their food down longer and longer. The sheer delight at being the cause of such happiness rewired their nervous systems. Those children wanted praise that much. So do we.

Whoever said 'flattery gets one nowhere' was a ... but I guess we should forgive them. Flattery, my friend, gets one everywhere!

How to be a VIP

In the first year of our monastery, I had to learn how to build. The first major structure was a six-toilet and six-shower ablution block, so I had to learn all about plumbing. In order to learn, I took the plans to a plumbing shop, laid the plans on the counter, and said, 'Help!'

It was quite a large order, so the man at the counter, Fred, didn't mind spending a little extra time explaining what parts were needed, why they were needed, and how to glue it all together. Eventually, with a lot of patience, commonsense, and advice from Fred, the waste-water plumbing was all finished. Our local council's health inspector came, gave it a stringent testing, and it passed. I was thrilled.

A few days later, the bill arrived for the plumbing parts. I asked for a cheque from our treasurer and sent it off with a letter of thanks, especially to Fred for helping us start our monastery.

I did not realise at the time that such a big plumbing firm, with many branches around Perth, had a separate accounts department. My letter was opened and read by a clerk in that section, who was so stunned at receiving a letter of praise that they took it immediately to the manager of accounts. Usually, when accounts receives a letter along with a cheque, it is a complaint. The head of the accounts department was also taken aback, and took my letter straight to the managing director of the whole company. The MD read the letter and was so pleased that he picked up the phone on his desk, rang Fred at the sales counter of one of their many branches, and told him about my letter on his mahogany desk.

'This is just the sort of thing we are looking for in our company, Fred. Customer relations! That's the way ahead.'

'Yes, Sir.'

'You've done an excellent job, Fred.'

'Yes, Sir.'

'I wish we had more employees like you.'

'Yes, Sir.'

'What salary are you on? Perhaps we can do better?'

'YES, SIR!'

'Well done, Fred!'

'Thank you, Sir.'

As it happened, I went into the plumbing shop an hour or two later to change a part for another job. There were two big Aussie plumbers, with shoulders as wide as septic tanks, waiting for service ahead of me. But Fred saw me. 'BRAHM!' he said with a big smile, 'Come here.'

I was given VIP treatment. I was taken around the back, where customers were not supposed to go, to choose the replacement part that I needed. Fred's mate at the counter told me about the recent phone call from the managing director.

I found the part that I needed. It was bigger and much more expensive than the part I was giving back. 'How much do we owe you?' I asked. 'What's the difference?'

With a smile from ear to ear, Fred replied, 'Brahm, for you, there's no difference!'

So praise makes good financial sense as well.

The two-finger smile

Praise saves us money, enriches our relationships and creates happiness. We need to spread more of it around.

The hardest person to give any praise to is ourself. I was brought up to believe that someone who praises themself becomes big-headed. That's not so. They become big-hearted. Praising our good qualities to ourself is positively encouraging them.

When I was a student, my first meditation teacher gave me some practical advice. He began by asking me the first thing I did after getting up in the morning.

'I go to the bathroom,' I said.

'Is there a mirror in your bathroom?' he enquired.

'Of course.'

'Good,' he said. 'Now, every morning, even before you brush your teeth, I want you to look in that mirror and smile at yourself.'

'Sir!' I began to protest. 'I am a student. Sometimes I go to bed very late, and get up in the morning not feeling my best. Some mornings, I would be frightened to look at myself in a mirror, let alone smile!'

He chuckled, looked me in the eye and said, 'If you cannot manage a natural smile, then take your two index fingers, place one on each corner of your mouth, and push up. Like this.' And he showed me.

He looked ridiculous. I giggled. He ordered me to try it. So I did.

The very next morning, I dragged myself out of bed and staggered to the bathroom. I looked at myself in the mirror. 'Urrgh!' It was not a pretty sight. A natural smile wasn't a goer. So I got out my two index fingers, placed one on each corner of my mouth and pushed up. I then saw this stupid young student making a silly face in the mirror, and I couldn't help grinning. Once there was a natural smile, I saw the student in the mirror smiling at me. So I smiled even more. The man in the mirror smiled even more. In a few seconds, we ended up laughing at each other.

I continued that practice every morning for two years. Every morning, no matter how I felt when I got out of bed, I was soon laughing at myself in the mirror, usually with the help of my two fingers. People say I smile a lot these days.

Perhaps the muscles around my mouth got kind of stuck in that position.

We can try the two-finger trick any time of the day. It is especially useful when we feel sick, fed up or downright depressed. Laughter has been proved to release endorphins into our bloodstream, which strengthens our immune system and make us feel happy.

It helps us see the 998 good bricks in our wall, not only the two bad bricks. And laughter makes us look beautiful. That's why I sometimes call our Perth Buddhist temple 'Ajahn Brahm's Beauty Salon'.

Priceless teachings

I was told that depression has spawned a multi-billion-dollar industry. That is really depressing! It doesn't seem right to grow rich from other people's suffering. In our austere tradition, the monks are not allowed to have money, and we never charge for the talks we give, for counselling, or for any other services.

An American woman rang up a fellow monk, a renowned teacher of meditation, to enquire about learning how to meditate.

'I hear you teach meditation,' she drawled over the phone.

'Yes, madam, I do,' he politely replied.

'How much do you charge?' she asked, getting to the point.

'Nothing, madam.'

'Then you can't be any good!' she replied, and she hung up the phone.

I received a similar phone call a few years ago from a Polish–Australian woman:

'Is there a talk at your centre this evening?' she enquired.

'Yes, madam. It starts at 8.00 p.m.,' I told her.

'How much do you have to pay?' she asked.

'Nothing, madam, it's free,' I explained. Then there was a pause.

'You haven't understood me,' she said forcefully. 'How much money do I have to give you to listen to the talk?'

'Madam, you don't have to give any money, it's free,' I said, as soothingly as I could.

'Listen!' she shouted at me down the line. 'Dollars! Cents! How much must I cough up to get in?'

'Madam, you don't have to cough up anything. You just walk in. Sit at the back, and leave whenever you like. No one will ask you for your name or address, you won't be handed any leaflets, and you won't be asked for any donation at the door. It's completely free.'

There was a long pause now.

Then she asked, sincerely wanting to know, 'Well, what do you guys get out of this then?'

'Happiness, madam,' I answered. 'Happiness.'

These days, when anyone asks how much these teachings cost, I never say they are free. I say they are priceless.

This too will pass

One of the most priceless of teachings that helps with depression, is also one of the simplest. But teachings that seem simple are easy to misunderstand. Only when we are finally free from depression can we claim to have truly understood the following story.

The new prisoner was afraid and very depressed. The stone walls of his cell soaked up any warmth; the hard iron bars sneered at all compassion; the jarring collision of steel, as many gates closed, locked hope beyond reach. His heart sank as low as his sentence stretched long. On the wall, by the head of his cot, he saw scratched in the stone the following words: THIS TOO WILL PASS.

These words pulled him through, as they must have supported the prisoner before him. No matter how hard it got, he would look at the inscription and remember, 'This too will pass.' On the day he was released, he knew the truth of those words. His time was completed; jail too had passed.

As he regained his life, he often thought about that message, writing it on bits of paper to leave by his bedside, in his car and at work. Even when times were bad, he never got depressed. He simply remembered, 'This too will pass', and struggled on through. The bad times never seemed to last all that long. Then when good times came he enjoyed them, but never too carelessly. Again he remembered, 'This too will pass', and so carried on working at his life, taking nothing for granted. The good times always seemed to last uncommonly long.

Even when he got cancer, 'This too will pass' gave him hope. Hope gave him strength and the positive attitude that beat the disease. One day the specialist confirmed that 'the cancer too had passed'.

At the end of his days, on his death bed, he whispered to his loved ones, 'This too will pass,' and settled easily into death. His words were his last gift of love to his family and friends. They learned from him that 'grief too will pass'.[5] Depression is a prison that many of us pass through.

'This too will pass' helps us pull through. It also avoids one of the great causes of depression, which is taking the happy times too much for granted.

The heroic sacrifice

When I was a schoolteacher, my attention was drawn to the student in my class of thirty who came bottom in the end-of-year exams. I could see that he was depressed as a result of his performance, so I took him aside.

I said to him: 'Someone has to come thirtieth in a class of thirty. This year, it happens to be you who has made the heroic sacrifice, so that none of your friends have to suffer the ignominy of being bottom of the class. You are so kind, so compassionate. You deserve a medal.'

We both knew that what I was saying was ridiculous, but he grinned. He didn't take it as such an end-of-the-world event any more.

He did much better the next year, when it was someone else's turn to make the heroic sacrifice.

A truck-load of dung

Unpleasant things, like coming bottom of our class, happen in life. They happen to everyone. The only difference between a happy person and one who gets depressed is how they respond to disasters.

Imagine you have just had a wonderful afternoon at the beach with a friend. When you return home, you find a huge truck-load of dung has been dumped right in front of your door. There are three things to know about this truck-load of dung:

1 You did not order it. It's not your fault.

2 You're stuck with it. No one saw who dumped it, so you cannot call anyone to take it away.

3 It is filthy and offensive, and its stench fills your whole house. It is almost impossible to endure.

In this metaphor, the truck-load of dung in front of the house stands for the traumatic experiences that are dumped on us in life. As with the truck-load of dung, there are three things to know about tragedy in our life:

1 We did not order it. We say 'Why me?'

2 We're stuck with it. No one, not even our best friends, can take it away (though they may try).

3 It is so awful, such a destroyer of our happiness, and its pain fills our whole life. It is almost impossible to endure.

There are two ways of responding to being stuck with a truck-load of dung. The first way is to carry the dung around with us. We put some in our pockets, some in our bags, and some up our shirts. We even put some down our pants. We find when we carry dung around, we lose a lot of friends! Even best friends don't seem to be around so often.

'Carrying around the dung' is a metaphor for sinking into depression, negativity or anger. It is a natural and understandable response to adversity. But we lose a lot of friends, because it is also natural and understandable that our friends don't like being around us when we're so depressed. Moreover, the pile of dung gets no less, but the smell gets worse as it ripens.

Fortunately, there's a second way. When we are dumped with a truck-load of dung, we heave a sigh, and then get down to work. Out come the wheelbarrow, the fork and the spade. We fork the dung into the barrow, wheel it around the back of the house, and dig it into the garden. This is tiring and difficult work, but we know there's no other option. Sometimes, all we can manage is half a barrow a day. We're doing something about the problem, rather than complaining our way into depression. Day after day we dig in the dung. Day after day, the pile gets smaller. Sometimes it takes several years, but the morning does come when we see that the dung in front of our house is all gone. Furthermore, a miracle has happened in another part of our house. The flowers in our garden are bursting out in a richness of colour all over the place. Their fragrance wafts down the street so that the neighbours, and even passers-by, smile in delight. Then the fruit tree in the corner is nearly falling over, it's so heavy with fruit. And the fruit is so sweet; you can't buy anything like it. There's so much of it that we are able to share it with our neighbours. Even passers-by get a delicious taste of the miracle fruit.

'Digging in the dung' is a metaphor for welcoming the tragedies as fertiliser for life. It is work that we have to do alone: no one can help us here. But by digging it into the garden of our heart, day by day, the pile of pain gets less. It may take us several years, but the morning does come when we see no more pain in our life and, in our heart, a miracle has happened. Flowers of kindness are bursting out all over the place, and the fragrance of love wafts way down our street, to our neighbours, to our relations and even to passers-by. Then our wisdom tree in the corner is bending down to us, loaded with sweet insights into the nature of life. We share those delicious fruits freely, even with the passers-by, without ever planning to.

When we have known tragic pain, learnt its lesson and grown our garden, then we can put our arms around another in deep tragedy and say, softly, 'I know.' They realise we do understand. Compassion begins. We show them the wheelbarrow, the fork and the spade, and boundless encouragement. If we haven't grown our own garden yet, this can't be done.

I have known many monks who are skilled in meditation, who are peaceful, composed and serene in adversity. But only a few have become great teachers. I often wondered why.

It seems to me now that those monks who had a relatively easy time of it, who had little dung to dig in, were the ones who didn't become teachers. It was the monks who had the enormous difficulties, dug them in quietly, and came through with a rich garden that became great teachers. They all had wisdom, serenity and compassion; but those with more dung had more to share with the world. My teacher, Ajahn Chah, who for me was the pinnacle of all teachers, must have had a whole trucking company line up with their dung at his door, in his early life.

Perhaps the moral of this story is that if you want to be of service to the world, if you wish to follow the path of compassion, then the next time a tragedy occurs in your life, you may say, 'Whoopee! More fertiliser for my garden!'

It's too much to hope for

It's too much to hope for a life without pain,
It's wrong to expect a life without pain,
For pain is our body's defence.
No matter how much we dislike it,
And nobody likes pain,
Pain is important,
And,
For pain we should be grateful!

How else would we know,
To move our hand from the fire?
Our finger from the blade?
Our foot from the thorn?
So pain is important,
And
For pain we should be grateful!

Yet, There's a type of pain that serves no purpose,
That's chronic pain,
It's that elite band of pain that's not for defence.
It's an attacking force.
An attacker from within
A destroyer of personal happiness
An aggressive assailant on personal ability
A ceaseless invader of personal peace
And,
A continuous harassment to life!

Chronic pain is the hardest hurdle for the mind to jump.
Sometimes it is almost impossible to jump,
Yet, we must keep trying,
And trying,
And trying,
Because if we don't it will destroy.

And,
From this battle will come some good,
The satisfaction of overcoming pain.
The achievement of happiness and peace,
of life in spite of it.
This is quite an achievement,
An achievement very special, very personal,
A feeling of strength
Of inner strength
Which has to be experienced to be understood.

So, we all have to accept pain,
Even sometimes destructive pain.
For it is part of the scheme of things,
And the mind can manage it,
And the mind will become stronger for the practice.

— Jonathan Wilson-Fuller

The reason for including this poem, with the kind permission of its author, is that it was written when Jonathan was only nine years old![6]

Being a dustbin

Part of my job is listening to people's problems. Monks are always good value for money, because they never charge anything. Often, when I hear the complex, sticky mess that some people get themselves into, my sympathy for them makes me depressed as well. To help a person out of a pit, I must sometimes enter the pit myself to reach for their hand—but I always remember to bring the ladder. After the session I am bright as always. My counselling work leaves no echoes, because of the way I was trained.

Ajahn Chah, my teacher in Thailand, said that monks must be dustbins. Monks, and senior monks especially, have to sit in their monastery, listen to people's problems and accept all their rubbish. Marital problems, difficulties with teenage children, rows with relations, financial problems—we hear the lot. I don't know why. What does a celibate monk know about marital problems? We left the world to get away from all that rubbish. But out of compassion we sit and listen, share our peace, and receive all the rubbish.

There was an extra, essential piece of advice that Ajahn Chah would give. He told us to be like a dustbin with a hole in the bottom! We were to receive all the rubbish, but not to keep any.

Therefore an effective friend, or counsellor, is like a dustbin with no bottom, and is never too full to listen to another problem.

Maybe it is fair!

Often in depression, we think: 'It's not fair! Why me?' It would ease matters a little if life was more just.

A middle-aged prisoner in my meditation class in jail asked to see me after the session. He'd been attending for several months and I'd got to know him quite well.

'Brahm,' he said, 'I wanted to tell you that I did not commit the crime for which I was locked up in this jail. I was innocent. I know many crims might say the same and be lying, but I am telling you the truth. I wouldn't lie to you, Brahm, not to you.' I believed him. The circumstance and his manner convinced me that he was telling the truth. I began to think how unfair this was, and wonder how I could mend this terrible injustice. But he interrupted my thoughts.

With a mischievous grin, he said, 'But Brahm, there were so many other crimes where I wasn't caught that I guess it is fair!'

I doubled up laughing. The old rogue had understood the law of karma, better even than some monks I knew.

How often is it that we do a 'crime', some hurtful, spiteful act, and we are not made to suffer for it? Do we ever say, 'It's not fair! Why wasn't I caught?'

When we are made to suffer for no apparent reason, though, we moan, 'It's not fair! Why me?' Perhaps it is fair. Like the prisoner in my story, perhaps there were so many other 'crimes' where we weren't caught that life is fair after all.

Critical Problems and their compassionate solutions

The law of karma

Most Westerners misunderstand the law of karma. They mistake it for fatalism, where one is doomed to suffer for some unknown crime in a forgotten past life. This is not quite so, as this story will show.

Two women were each baking a cake.

The first woman had miserable ingredients. The old white flour had to have the green mouldy bits removed first. The cholesterol-enriched butter was almost going rancid. She had to pick the brown lumps out of the white sugar (because someone had put in a spoon wet with coffee), and the only fruit she had were ancient sultanas, as hard as depleted uranium. And her kitchen was of the style called 'pre-World War'—which World War was a matter of debate.

The second woman had the very best of ingredients. The organically grown whole-wheat flour was guaranteed GM free. She had cholesterol-free margarine, raw sugar and succulent fruit grown in her own garden. And her kitchen was 'state-of-the-art', with every modern gadget.

Which woman baked the more delicious of cakes? It is often not the person with the best ingredients who bakes the better cake—there is more to baking a cake than just the ingredients. Sometimes the person with miserable ingredients puts so much effort, care and love into their baking that their cake comes out the most delicious of all. It is what we do with the ingredients that counts.

I have some friends who have had miserable ingredients to work with in this life: they were born into poverty, possibly abused as children, not clever at school, maybe disabled and unable to play sport. But the few qualities they did have they put together so well that they baked a mightily impressive cake. I admire them greatly. Do you recognise such people?

I have other friends who have had wonderful ingredients to work with in this life. Their families were wealthy and loving, they were intelligent at school, talented at sport, good looking and popular, and yet they wasted their young lives with drugs or alcohol. Do you recognise such a one?

Half of karma is the ingredients we have got to work with. The other half, the most crucial part, is what we make of them in this life.

Drinking tea when there's no way out

There is always something we can do with the ingredients of our day, even if that something is just sitting down, enjoying our last cup of tea. The following story was told to me by a fellow schoolteacher, who had served in the British Army in World War II.

He was on patrol in the jungles of Burma; he was young, far from home and very frightened. The scout from his patrol returned to tell the captain the terrible news. Their small patrol had stumbled into a huge number of Japanese troops. The patrol was vastly outnumbered and completely surrounded. The young British soldier prepared himself to die.

He expected his captain to order the men to fight their way out: that was the manly thing to do. Maybe someone would make it. If not, well, they would take some of the enemy with them into death; that's what soldiers did.

But not the soldier who was the captain. He ordered his men to stay put, sit down, and make a cup of tea. It was the British Army, after all!

The young soldier thought his commanding officer had gone mad. How can anyone think of a cup of tea when surrounded by the enemy, with no way out and about to die? In an army, especially at war, orders had to be obeyed. They all made what they thought was to be their last cup of tea. Before they had finished drinking their tea, the scout came back and whispered to his captain. The captain asked for the men's attention. 'The enemy has moved,' he announced. 'There is now a way out. Pack your kit quickly, and quietly—let's go!'

They all got out safely, which is why he could tell me the story many years later. He told me that he owed his life to the wisdom of that captain, not just at war in Burma, but many times since. Several times in his life, it was as if he was surrounded by the enemy, completely outnumbered, with no way out and about to die. He meant by 'the enemy' serious illness, horrendous difficulty and tragedy, in the middle of which there seemed no way out. Without the experience in Burma, he would have tried to fight his way through the problem, and no doubt made it much worse. But instead, when death or deadly trouble surrounded him on all sides, he simply sat down and made a cup of tea.

The world is always changing; life is a flux. He drank his tea, conserved his powers and waited for the time, which always came, when he could do something effective, like escape.

For those who don't like tea, remember this saying: 'When there's nothing to do, then do nothing.'

It may seem obvious, but it may also save your life.

Going with the flow

A wise monk, whom I have known for many years, was hiking with an old friend in an antipodean wilderness. Late one hot afternoon they arrived at a splendid stretch of isolated beach. Even though it is against the monks' rules to swim just for fun, the blue water was inviting and he needed to cool off after the long walk, so he stripped off and went for a swim.

When he was a young layman, he had been a strong swimmer. But now, as a monk of long standing, it had been many years since he had last swum. After only a couple of minutes of splashing in the surf, he was caught in a strong rip-tide that began to sweep him out to sea. He was later told that this was a very dangerous beach because of the fierce currents.

At first, the monk tried to swim against the current. He soon realised, though, that the force of the current was too strong for him. His training now came to his aid. He relaxed, let go and went with the flow.

It was an act of great courage to relax in such a situation, as he saw the shoreline recede further and further away. He was many hundreds of metres away from land when the current diminished. Only then did he start to swim away from the riptide and back towards shore.

He told me that the swim back to land took every last ounce of his energy reserves. He reached the beach utterly exhausted. He was certain that, had he tried to fight the current, it would have beaten him. He would have been swept far out to sea just the same, but so depleted in energy that he wouldn't have made it back. If he hadn't let go and gone with the flow, he was sure he would have drowned.

Such anecdotes demonstrate that the adage 'When there's nothing to do, then do nothing' is not fanciful theory. Rather, it can be life-saving wisdom. Whenever the current is stronger than you are, that is the time to go with the flow. When you are able to be effective, that is the time to put forth effort.

Caught between a tiger and a snake

There is an old Buddhist story which describes in much the same way as the story above how we might respond to life or death crises.

A man was being chased by a tiger in the jungle. Tigers can run much faster than a man, and they eat men too. The tiger was hungry; the man was in trouble.

With the tiger almost upon him, the man saw a well by the side of the path. In desperation, he leapt in. As soon as he had committed himself to the leap, he saw what a big mistake he had made. The well was dry and, at its bottom, he could see the coils of a big black snake.

Instinctively, his arm reached for the side of the well, where his hand found the root of a tree. The root checked his fall. When he had gathered his senses, he looked down to see the black snake raise its head to full height and try to strike him on his feet; but his feet were a fraction too high. He looked up to see the tiger leaning into the well trying to paw him from above; but his hand holding the root was a fraction too low. As he contemplated his dire predicament, he saw two mice, one white and one black, emerge from a small hole and begin chewing on the root.

As the tiger was attempting to paw at the man, its hind-quarters were rubbing against a small tree, making it shake. On a branch of that tree, overhanging the well, was a beehive. Honey began to drop into the well. The man put out his tongue and caught some.

'Mmmm! That tastes good,' he said to himself and smiled.

This story, as it is traditionally told, ends there. That is why it is so true to life. Life, like those long-running TV soaps, doesn't have a neat ending. Life is forever in the process of completion.

Moreover, often in our life it is as if we are caught between a hungry tiger and a big black snake, between death and something worse, with day and night (the two mice) chewing away at our precarious grip on life. Even in such dire situations, there is always some honey dripping from somewhere. If we are wise, we will put out our tongue and enjoy some of that honey. Why not? When there's nothing to do, then do nothing, and enjoy some of life's honey.

As I said, the story traditionally ends there. However, in order to make a point, I usually tell my audience the true ending. This is what happened next.

As the man was enjoying the honey, the mice were chewing the root thinner and thinner, the big black snake was stretching closer and closer to the man's feet, and the tiger was leaning so its paw was almost reaching the man's hand. Then the tiger leant too far. It tumbled into the well, missing the man, crushing the snake to death, and dying itself in the fall.

Well, it could happen! And something unexpected usually does happen. That's our life. So why waste the moments of honey, even in the most desperate of troubles. The future is uncertain. We never can be sure of what's coming next.

Advice for life

In the story above, with the tiger and snake both dead, it was time for the man to do something. He stopped tasting the honey and, with effort, climbed out of the well and walked out of the jungle into safety. Life is not always doing nothing, tasting honey.

A young man from Sydney told me that he had once met my teacher, Ajahn Chah, in Thailand, and received the best advice of his life.

Many young Westerners interested in Buddhism had heard of Ajahn Chah by the early 1980s. This young man decided to make the long journey to Thailand, for the sole reason of meeting the great monk and asking some questions.

It is a long journey. Having arrived in Bangkok, eight hours from Sydney, he took the overnight train, ten hours to Ubon. There he negotiated a taxi to take him to Wat Nong Pah Pong, Ajahn Chah's monastery. Tired but excited, he finally reached Ajahn Chah's hut.

The teacher was famous. He was sitting under his hut, as usual, surrounded by a large crowd of monks and generals, poor farmers and rich merchants, village women in rags and decorated ladies from Bangkok, all sitting side by side. There was no discrimination under Ajahn Chah's hut.

The Australian sat down on the edge of the large crowd. Two hours passed and Ajahn Chah hadn't even noticed him. There were too many others ahead of him. Despondent, he got up and walked away.

On the way through the monastery to the main gate, he saw some monks sweeping leaves by the bell tower. It was another hour before his taxi was due to meet him at the gate, so he too picked up a broom, thinking to make some good karma.

Some thirty minutes later, while busily sweeping, he felt someone putting their hand on his shoulder. He turned around to see, shocked and delighted, that the hand belonged to Ajahn Chah, who stood smiling before him.

Ajahn Chah had seen the Westerner, but had no chance to address him. The great monk was now on his way out of the monastery to another appointment, so he had paused in front of the young man from Sydney to give him a gift. Ajahn Chah said something quickly in Thai, then walked off to his appointment.

A translator–monk told him, 'Ajahn Chah says that if you are going to sweep, give it everything you've got.' Then the translator left to join Ajahn Chah.

The young man thought about that brief teaching on the long journey back to Australia. He realised, of course, that Ajahn Chah was teaching him much more than how to sweep leaves. The meaning became clear to him.

'Whatever you are doing, give it everything you've got.'

He told me back in Australia several years later that this 'advice for life' was worth a hundred such journeys to distant parts. It was now his creed, and it had brought him happiness and success. When he was working, he'd give it everything he'd got. When he was resting, he'd give it everything he'd got. When he was socialising, he'd give it everything he'd got. It was a formula for success. Oh, and when he was doing nothing, he'd give nothing everything he'd got.

Is there a problem?

The French philosopher–mathematician Blaise Pascal (1623–62) once said: 'All the troubles of man come from his not knowing how to sit still.'

I would add to this '... and not knowing when to sit still.'

In 1967, Israel was at war with Egypt, Syria and Jordan. In the midst of what became known as the Six Day War, a reporter asked the former British Prime Minister, Harold Macmillan, what he thought about the problem in the Middle East.

Without hesitation, the then elder statesman answered, 'There is no problem in the Middle East.' The reporter was stunned. 'What do you mean, "There is no problem in the Middle East"?' the reporter demanded to know. 'Don't you know there's a vicious war going on? Don't you realise that as we are speaking, bombs are falling from the sky, tanks are blowing each other up, and soldiers are being sprayed with bullets? Many people are dead or wounded. What do you mean, "There is no problem in the Middle East"?'

The experienced statesman patiently explained. 'Sir, a problem is something with a solution. There is no solution to the Middle East. Therefore it can't be a problem.'

How much time do we waste in our lives worrying about things that, at the time, have no solution, so aren't a problem?

Making decisions

A problem with a solution needs a decision. But how do we make the important decisions in our life? Usually we try to get someone else to make the difficult decisions for us. That way, if it goes wrong, we've got someone to blame. Some of my friends try to trick me into making decisions for them, but I won't. All I will do is show them how they can make wise decisions by themselves.

When we come to the crossroads and we are unsure what direction to take, we should pull over to the side, have a break and wait for a bus. Soon, usually when we are not expecting it, a bus arrives. On the front of a public bus is a sign in big bold letters indicating where the bus is going. If that destination suits you, then take that bus. If not, wait. There's always another bus behind.

In other words, when we have to make a decision and are unsure what that decision should be, we need to pull over to the side, have a break and wait. Soon, usually when we are not expecting it, a solution will come. Every solution has its own destination. If that destination suits us, then we take that solution. If not, we wait. There's always another solution coming behind.

That's how I make my decisions. I gather all the information and wait for the solution. A good one will always come, as long as I am patient. It usually arrives unexpectedly, when I am not thinking about it.

Blaming others

When attempting to make important decisions you may choose to use the strategy suggested in the previous story. But you don't have to follow this method. It's your decision after all. So if it doesn't work, don't blame me.

A university student came to see one of our monks. She had an important exam the following day and wanted the monk to do some chanting for her, to bring her good luck. The monk kindly obliged, thinking it would give her confidence. It was all free of charge. She gave no donation.

We never saw the young woman again. But I heard from her friends that she was going around saying that the monks in our temple were no good, that we didn't know how to chant properly. She had failed her exam.

Her friends told me that she had failed because she had hardly done any study. She was a party girl. She had hoped that the monks would take care of the 'less important', academic part of university life.

It may seem satisfying to blame someone else when something goes wrong in our life, but blaming others rarely solves the problem.

A man had an itch on his bum. He scratched his head. The itch never went away.

That is how Ajahn Chah described blaming others, like having an itch on your bum and scratching your head.

The Emperor's three questions

I had received an invitation to give the keynote address at an education seminar in Perth. I wondered why. When I arrived at the function centre a woman, whose name tag showed she was the organiser of the seminar, approached to welcome me. 'Do you remember me?' she asked.

That is one of the most dangerous questions to answer. I chose to be blunt and said, 'No.'

She smiled and told me that seven years previously I had given a talk at the school of which she was the principal. A story that I had told at her school changed the direction of her career. She resigned as principal. She then worked tirelessly to set up a program for the kids who had dropped out of the system—street kids, underage prostitutes, drug addicts—to give them another chance, tailored to their situation. My story, she told me, was the philosophy underpinning her program. The story has been adapted from a book of short stories compiled by Leo Tolstoy that I read as a student.[7]

Long ago, an Emperor sought a philosophy of life. He needed wisdom to guide his rule and govern himself. The religions and philosophies of the time did not satisfy him. So he searched for his philosophy in the experience of life.

Eventually, he realised that he required the answers to only three fundamental questions. With those answers, he would have all the wise guidance he needed. The three questions were:

1 When is the most important time?

2 Who is the most important person?

3 What is the most important thing to do?

After a long search, which took up most of the original story, he found the three answers on a visit to a hermit. What do you think the answers are? Look at the questions again, please. Pause, before you read on.

We all know the answer to the first question, but we forget it too often. The most important time is 'now' of course. That is the only time we ever have. So if you want to tell your Mum or Dad how much you really love them, how grateful you are for them being your parents, do so now. Not tomorrow. Not in five minutes. Now. In five minutes it is often too late. If you need to say sorry to your partner, don't start thinking of all the reasons why you shouldn't. Just do it right now. The opportunity may never come again. Grab the moment.

The answer to the second question is powerfully profound. Few people ever guess the correct answer. When I read the answer as a student, it had me spinning for days. It saw deeper into the question than I'd ever imagined. The answer is that the most important person is the one you are with.

I recalled asking questions of college professors and not being fully heard. They were outwardly listening, but inwardly wanting me to go. They had more important things to do. That's what I felt. It was a rotten feeling. I also recalled rousing my courage to approach a famous lecturer and ask a personal question, and being surprised and so pleased that he was giving me his total attention. Other professors were waiting to speak with him, I was a mere long-haired student, but he made me feel important. The difference was huge.

Communication, and love, can only be shared when the one you are with, *no matter who they are,* is the most important person in the world for you, at that time. They feel it. They know it. They respond.

Married couples often complain that their partner doesn't really listen to them. What they mean is that their partner doesn't make them feel important anymore. Divorce lawyers would have to look for other work if every person in a relationship remembered the answer to the Emperor's second question and put it into practice, so that no matter how tired or busy we are, when we are with our partner, we make them feel as though they are the most important person in the world.

In business, where the person we are with is a potential customer, if we treat them as the most important person for us at that time, our sales will go up and with it our salary.

The Emperor in the original story escaped assassination by fully listening to the advice of a small boy on his way to visit the hermit. When a powerful Emperor is with a mere child, that boy is the most important person in the world for him, and saves the Emperor's life. When friends come up to me after a long day to tell me about their problems, I remember the answer to the Emperor's second question and give them total importance. It is selflessness. Compassion supplies the energy, and it works.

The organiser of the education seminar had, in her first interviews with the children she was reaching out to help, practised 'the most important person is the one you are with'. For many of those kids, it was the first time they were made to feel important, especially by an influential adult. Moreover, by giving them importance, she was fully listening, not judging. The kids were heard. The program was tailored accordingly. The kids felt respected, and it worked. Mine wasn't to be the keynote speech after all. One of the kids got up to speak after me. He related his story of family trouble, drugs and crime, of how the program returned hope to his life, and how he was soon to go to university. I was wet-eyed by the end. That was the keynote address.

Most of the time in your life you are by yourself. Then, the most important person, the one you are with, is you. There is plenty of time to give importance to yourself. Who is the first person you are aware of when you wake up in the morning? You! Do you ever say, 'Good morning, me. Have a nice day!'? I do. Who is the last person you are aware of when you go to sleep? Yourself again! I say good night to myself. I give myself importance in the many private moments of my day. It works.

The answer to the Emperor's third question, 'What is the most important thing to do?' is to care. 'To care' brings together being careful and caring. The answer illustrates that it is where we are coming from that is the most important thing. Before describing what it means to care, using several stories, I will summarise the three questions of the Emperor, together with the answers:

1 When is the most important time? Now.

2 Who is the important person? The person you are with.

3 What is the most important thing to do? To care.

The cow that cried

I arrived early to lead my meditation class in a low-security prison. A crim who I had never seen before was waiting to speak with me. He was a giant of a man with bushy hair and beard and tattooed arms; the scars on his face told me he'd been in many a violent fight. He looked so fearsome that I wondered why he was coming to learn meditation. He wasn't the type. I was wrong of course.

He told me that something had happened a few days before that had spooked the hell out of him. As he started speaking, I picked up his thick Ulster accent. To give me some background, he told me that he had grown up in the violent streets of Belfast. His first stabbing was when he was seven years old. The school bully had demanded the money he had for his lunch. He said no. The older boy took out a long knife and asked for the money a second time. He thought the bully was bluffing. He said no again. The bully never asked a third time, he just plunged the knife into the seven-year-old's arm, drew it out and walked away.

He told me that he ran in shock from the schoolyard, with blood streaming down his arm, to his father's house close by. His unemployed father took one look at the wound and led his son into their kitchen, but not to dress the wound. The father opened a drawer, took out a big kitchen knife, gave it to his son, and ordered him to go back to school and stab the boy back.

That was how he had been brought up. If he hadn't grown so big and strong, he would have been long dead.

The jail was a prison farm where short-term prisoners, or long-term prisoners close to release, could be prepared for life outside, some by learning a trade in the farming industry. Furthermore, the produce from the prison farm would supply all the prisons around Perth with inexpensive food, thus keeping down costs. Australian farms grow cows, sheep and pigs, not just wheat and vegetables; so did the prison farm. But unlike other farms, the prison farm had its own slaughterhouse, on-site.

Every prisoner had to have a job in the prison farm. I was informed by many of the inmates that the most sought-after jobs were in the slaughterhouse. These jobs were especially popular with violent offenders. And the most sought-after job of all, which you had to fight for, was the job of the slaughterer himself. That giant and fearsome Irishman was the slaughterer.

He described the slaughterhouse to me. Super-strong stainless steel railings, wide at the opening, narrowed down to a single channel inside the building, just wide enough for one animal to pass through at a time. Next to the narrow channel, raised on a platform, he would stand with the electric gun. Cows, pigs or sheep would be forced into the stainless steel funnel using dogs and cattle prods. He said they would always scream, each in its own way, and try to escape. They could smell death, hear death, feel death. When an animal was alongside his platform, it would be writhing and wriggling and moaning in full voice. Even though his gun could kill a large bull with a single high-voltage charge, the animal would never stand still long enough for him to aim properly. So it was one shot to stun, next shot to kill. One shot to stun, next shot to kill. Animal after animal. Day after day.

The Irishman started to become excited as he moved to the occurrence, only a few days before, that had unsettled him so much. He started to swear. In what followed, he kept repeating, 'This is God's f…ing truth!' He was afraid I wouldn't believe him.

That day they needed beef for the prisons around Perth. They were slaughtering cows. One shot to stun, next shot to kill. He was well into a normal day's killing when a cow came up like he had never seen before. This cow was silent. There wasn't even a whimper. Its head was down as it walked purposely, voluntarily, slowly into position next to the platform. It did not writhe or wriggle or try to escape.

Once in position, the cow lifted her head and stared at her executioner, absolutely still.

The Irishman hadn't seen anything even close to this before. His mind went numb with confusion. He couldn't lift his gun; nor could he take his eyes away from the eyes of the cow. The cow was looking right inside him.

He slipped into timeless spaces. He couldn't tell me how long it took, but as the cow held him in eye contact, he noticed something that shook him even more. Cows have very big eyes. He saw in the left eye of the cow, above the lower eyelid, water begin to gather. The amount of water grew and grew, until it was too much for the eyelid to hold. It began to trickle slowly all the way down her cheek, forming a glistening line of tears. Long-closed doors were opening slowly to his heart. As he looked in disbelief, he saw in the right eye of the cow, above the lower eyelid, more water gathering, growing by the moment, until it too, was more than the eyelid could contain. A second stream of water trickled slowly down her face. And the man broke down. The cow was crying.

He told me that he threw down his gun, swore to the full extent of his considerable capacity to the prison officers, that they could do whatever they liked to him, 'BUT THAT COW AIN'T DYING!'

He ended by telling me he was a vegetarian now.

That story was true. Other inmates of the prison farm confirmed it for me. The cow that cried taught one of the most violent of men what it means to care.

The little girl and her friend

I told the story of the cow that cried to a group of senior citizens in a country town in the southwest of Western Australia. One of the old men told me a similar story, from his youth, in the early part of last century.

His friend's daughter was around four or five years old. One morning, she asked her Mum for a saucer of milk. Her busy mother was pleased that her daughter wanted to drink milk, so didn't think much about why she wanted it in a saucer, rather than in a glass.

The following day, around the same time, the little girl asked for a saucer of milk again. Mum gladly obliged. Children like to play games with their food; the mother was just glad her daughter wanted to drink something healthy.

The same happened, at the same time, for the next few days. The mother never actually saw her daughter drink the saucer of milk, so she began to wonder what the child was up to. She decided to secretly follow the little girl.

In those days, nearly all the houses were raised off the ground on stumps. The little girl went outside the house, knelt down next to the side of the building, put down the saucer of milk, and softly called out into the dark spaces underneath the house. In a few moments, out came a huge black tiger snake. It began drinking the milk, with the little girl smiling only a few inches away. The mother could do nothing; her child was too close. In terror she watched until the snake finished the milk and went back under the house. That evening, she told her husband on his return from work. He told his wife to give their daughter a saucer of milk again tomorrow. He would fix things.

At the same time the next day, the little girl asked her Mum for a saucer of milk. She took the saucer of milk outside as usual, placed it next to the side of the house, and called out for her friend. As soon as the big tiger snake appeared from out of the darkness, there was the cracking explosion of a gun close by. The force of the bullet threw the tiger snake against one of the house stumps, splitting apart its head in front of the girl. Her father stood up from behind one of the bushes, and put away his gun.

From that time on, the little girl refused to eat. In the old man's words, 'She started fretting.' Nothing the parents could do would make her eat. She had to go to the district hospital. They couldn't help her either. The little girl died.

The father might just as well have shot his little girl, when he blasted to death her friend, in front of her eyes.

I asked the old man who told me that story whether he thought that tiger snake would ever have harmed that little girl?

'Not bloody likely!' replied the old digger.

I agreed, but not in the same words.

The snake, the mayor and the monk

I spent more than eight years as a monk in Thailand. Most of that time I was in forest monasteries, living among snakes. When I arrived in 1974, I was told that in Thailand there are a hundred species of snke: ninety-nine are venomous—their bite will kill you—and the other one will strangle you to death!

During this time I saw snakes almost every day. Once I stepped on a six-foot snake in my hut. We both jumped, fortunately in opposite directions. I even peed on a snake early one morning, thinking it was a stick. I apologised, of course. (Perhaps the snake thought it was being blessed with holy water.) And once while I was chanting at a ceremony a snake crawled up the back of one of the other monks. Only when it reached his shoulder did the monk turn around to look; and the snake turned to look at him. I stopped chanting and for a few ridiculous seconds the monk and the snake were eyeballing each other. The monk carefully flicked off his robe, the snake slithered away, and we carried on with the chanting.

We were trained as forest monks to develop loving-kindness for all creatures, especially snakes. We cared for their welfare. That is why, in those days, no monk would ever be bitten.

I saw two huge snakes while I was in Thailand. The first was a python at least seven metres long with a body as thick as my thigh. When you see something that size, you stop in disbelief; but it was real. I saw it again a few years later and many other monks in that monastery also saw it. I have been told it is now dead. The other huge snake was a king cobra. It was on one of the three occasions living in Thai rainforests when I felt the atmosphere become electric, the hairs stand up on my neck and my senses suddenly become inexplicably acute. I turned a corner of the jungle path to see a thick black snake blocking the 1.5-metre-wide path. I could not see its head or its tail: both were in the bushes. And it was moving. By following its movement, I counted the length of that snake in path widths. It took seven path widths until I saw the tail. That snake was over 10 metres long! I saw it. I told the local villagers. They told me it was a king cobra—a big one.

A Thai monk disciple of Ajahn Chah, now a famous teacher in his own right, was meditating in the Thai jungle with a number of monks. The sounds of an approaching creature caused them all to open their eyes. They saw a king cobra coming towards them. In some parts of Thailand the king cobra also bears the name 'one step snake', because after it strikes you all you have left is one step, and then death! The king cobra came up to the senior monk, raised its head level with the monk's head, opened its hood and began spitting, 'Hsss! Hsss!'

What would you do? It would be a waste of time running. Those big snakes can go much faster than you can.

What the Thai monk did was to smile, gently raise his right hand, and softly pat the king cobra on the top of its head, saying in Thai, 'Thank you for coming to visit me.' All the monks saw that.

This was a special monk with exceptional kindness. The king cobra stopped hissing, closed its hood, lowered its head to the ground, and went to see one of the other monks, 'Hsss! Hsss!'

That monk said later that no way was he going to try patting a king cobra on the head! He froze. He was terrified. He was silently wishing the king cobra would quickly go off and visit one of the other monks.

That cobra-patting Thai monk once stayed several months at our monastery in Australia. We were building our main hall and had several other building projects waiting for approval at our local council's offices. The mayor of the local council came for a visit to see what we were doing.

The mayor was certainly the most influential man in the district. He had grown up in the area and was a successful farmer. He was also a neighbour. He came in a nice suit, befitting his position as mayor. The jacket was unbuttoned, revealing a very large, Australian-size stomach, which strained at the shirt buttons and bulged over the top of his best trousers. The Thai monk, who could speak no English, saw the mayor's stomach. Before I could stop him, he went over to the mayor and started patting it. 'Oh no!' I thought. 'You can't go patting a Lord Mayor on the stomach like that. Our building plans will never be approved now. We're done! Our monastery is finished.'

The more that Thai monk, with a gentle grin, patted and rubbed the mayor's big stomach, the more the mayor began to smile and giggle. In a few seconds, the dignified mayor was gurgling like a baby. He obviously loved every minute of having his stomach rubbed and patted by this extraordinary Thai monk.

All our building plans were approved. And the mayor became one of our best friends and helpers.

The most essential part of caring is where we're coming from. That Thai monk was coming from such a pure heart that he could pat king cobras on the head, and mayors on the stomach, and they both loved it. I would not recommend that you try this. At least not until you can care like a saint.

The bad snake

The final snake-tale in this book is an adaptation of an old Buddhist Jataka story. It shows that 'to care' does not always mean to be meek, mild and passive.

A bad snake lived in a forest outside a village. He was vicious, malicious and mean. He would bite people just for fun—his fun, that is. When the bad snake became advanced in snake-years, he began to wonder what happens to snakes when they die. All his hissing life he had spat scorn on religions and those snakes that, in his opinion, were gullible and susceptible to such nonsense. Now he was interested.

Not far from the snake's hole, on the top of a hill, lived a holy snake. All holy people live on the summit of a hill or mountain, even holy snakes. It's the tradition. One never hears of a holy man living in a swamp.

One day, the bad snake decided to visit the holy snake. He put on a raincoat, dark glasses and hat so his friends wouldn't recognise him. Then he slithered up the hill to the monastery of the holy snake. He arrived during the middle of a sermon. The holy snake was sitting on a rock with hundreds of snakes listening with rapt attention. Bad snake slithered to the edge of the throng, close to an exit, and began to listen.

The more he listened, the more sense it made. He started to become convinced, then inspired and then, finally, converted. After the sermon, he went up to holy snake, tearfully confessed the many sins of his life, and promised, from now on, he'd be a totally different snake. He vowed in front of holy snake never to bite a human again. He was going to be kind. He was going to be caring. He was going to teach other snakes how to be good. He even left a donation in the box on the way out (when everyone was looking, of course).

Although snakes can talk to snakes, it all sounds like one and the same hiss to human beings. Bad snake, or formerly bad snake, was unable to tell the people that he was now a pacifist. Villagers would still avoid him, even though they began to wonder about the Amnesty International badge he wore so prominently on his chest. Then one day a villager, distracted by a song on his Walkman, danced right past bad snake, and bad snake didn't strike; he just smiled religiously.

From that time on, the villagers realised that bad snake was no longer dangerous. They would walk right past him as he sat cross-coiled in meditation outside his hole. Then some naughty boys from the village came to tease him.

'Hey, you slimy creep!' they jeered from a safe distance. 'Show us your fangs, if you've got any, you oversized worm. You're a wimp, a cream-puff, a disgrace to your species!'

He didn't like being called a slimy creep, even though there was some truth in the description, or an oversized worm. But how could he defend himself? He had vowed not to bite.

Seeing that the snake was now passive, the boys grew bolder and threw stones and clods of earth. They laughed when a stone hit. The snake knew that he was fast enough to bite any one of those boys, before you could finish saying 'World Wildlife Fund'. But his vow prevented him. So the boys came closer and started hitting him over the back with sticks. The snake took the painful beating; but he realised that, in the real world, you had to be mean to protect yourself. Religion was nonsense after all. So he slithered painfully up the hill to see that fake of a snake, and be released from his vow.

Holy snake saw him coming, all battered and bruised, and asked, 'What happened to you?'

'It's all your fault,' bad snake complained bitterly.

'What do you mean, "It's all my fault"?' protested the holy snake.

'You told me not to bite. Now look what's happened to me! Religion might work in a monastery, but in the real world ...'

'Oh you stupid snake!' holy snake interrupted. 'Oh you foolish snake! Oh you idiot snake! It's true that I told you not to bite. But I never told you not to hiss, did I?'

Sometimes in life, even saints have to 'hiss' to be kind. But no one needs to bite.

Wisdom and inner silence

The wings of compassion

If kindness is imagined as a beautiful dove, then wisdom is its wings. Compassion without wisdom never takes off.

A boy scout performed his good deed for the day by guiding an old lady across a busy road. The trouble was, she didn't want to go; she felt too embarrassed to tell him.

That story, unfortunately, describes well much that goes by the name of compassion in our world. We assume, too often, that we know what the other person needs.

A young man, born deaf, was visiting his doctor accompanied by his parents for a regular check-up. The doctor excitedly told his parents about a new medical procedure, which he had just read about in a medical journal. In ten per cent of people born deaf, full hearing can be restored through a simple, inexpensive operation. He asked the parents if they wanted to give it a try. They quickly said yes.

That young man was one of the ten per cent whose hearing was fully restored. And he was so angry and upset with both his parents and the doctor. He hadn't heard what they were discussing at his regular check-up. No one asked him if he wanted to hear. Now he complained that he had to endure the constant torment of noise, which he could make little sense of. He never wanted to hear in the first place.

The parents and the doctor, and myself before I read this story, assumed that everyone would want to hear. We knew best. Compassion that carries such assumptions is foolish and dangerous. It causes so much suffering in the world.

Caring for a son

The trouble with parents is that they always think they know best what their child needs. Often they get it wrong. Sometimes they get it right, as did the Chinese poet Su Tung P'o (1036–1101 CE) almost a thousand years ago when he wrote the following poem:

On the birth of my son

Families, when a child is born
Want it to be intelligent.
I, through intelligence,
Having wrecked my whole life,
Only hope the baby will prove ignorant and stupid.
Then he will crown a tranquil life,
By becoming a Cabinet Minister.

What is wisdom?

While still a student, I would spend most of my summer vacations walking and camping in the highlands of Scotland. I delighted in the solitude, beauty and peace of the Scottish mountains.

One memorable afternoon, I was ambling by the ocean along a narrow road, which wound along the headlands and inlets of the far north. The warm, bright sun was like a spotlight for the extraordinary beauty around me. The moorland was an endless sweep of velvety grass in the fresh green of springtime; the cliffs had been sculpted like cathedrals soaring high above the swirling sea; the ocean was the blue of late evening, as if scattered with fairy lights sparkling and twinkling in the sunrays; and small green and brown rock islands seemed to surf on the waves as far as the haze-line of the horizon. Even the gulls and the terns were gliding and wheeling—in euphoria, I was certain. It was nature showing its finest, in one of the most scenic parts of our world, on a day of sunny glory.

I was skipping along in spite of my heavy back pack. I was joyous, without a care, high on the inspiration from nature. Ahead of me, I saw a small car parked by the roadside next to the cliff. Immediately, I imagined that its driver had also been overcome by the beauty of the day here and had stopped to drink its ambrosia. When I was close enough to the car to see through its back window, I was disappointed and dismayed. The single occupant of that vehicle, a middle-aged man, was reading a newspaper.

The newspaper was so big, it blocked the whole view of the world around him. Instead of seeing ocean and cliff and island and grassland, all he could see was war and politics and scandals and sport. That newspaper was wide, yet very thin. Only a few millimetres on the other side of that black dreary newsprint lay the pure rainbow-coloured elation of nature. I thought to take out a pair of scissors from my pack, and cut a small hole in his newspaper, so he could see what was on the other side of the article on the economy he was reading. But he was a big hairy Scotsman, and I was a scrawny underfed student. I left him to read about the world, while I danced on into it.

Our minds are mostly occupied with the sort of stuff that fills newspapers: wars in our relationships, politics in family and at work, personal scandals which upset us so, and the sport of our carnal pleasures. If we do not know how to put down that 'newspaper in our mind' from time to time, if that is what we are obsessed with, if that is all we know—then we will never experience the unsullied joy and peace of nature at is finest. We will never know wisdom.

Eating wisely

Some of my friends enjoy dining out. Some evenings they go to very expensive restaurants, where they are prepared to spend a lot of money on exquisite food. However, they waste the experience by neglecting the taste of the food and concentrating on the conversation they are having with their partner.

Who would talk during a concert given by a great orchestra? Chatter would hinder your enjoyment of the beautiful music, and would probably get you thrown out. Even when watching a great movie, we hate being distracted. So why do people engage in chitchat when they dine out?

If the restaurant is mediocre, then it may be a good idea to start a conversation to take your mind off the insipid meal. But when the food is really delicious, and very costly, telling your partner to be quiet so you can get your full money's worth is eating wisely.

Even when we do eat in silence, we often fail to savour the moment. Instead, while we are chewing on one piece of food, our attention is distracted as we look at our plate to choose the next thing on our fork. Some are even two or three forkfuls ahead of themselves—one forkful is in the mouth, one is waiting on the fork, another is heaped up waiting on the plate, while the mind contemplates the morsel coming third on the fork.

In order to relish the taste of your food, and know life in its fullness, we should often savour one moment at a time in silence. Then we might get our money's worth in the five-star restaurant called life.

Solving the problem

As a Buddhist monk, I often get to talk live on radio shows. I should have been more cautious about accepting a recent invitation to a radio station one night. Only after I entered the studio was I told that the show was to be on 'adult themes', and that I would be taking live questions, together with a well-known, professional sexologist!

Once we got over the problem of pronouncing my name on air (we agreed that I would be called 'Mr. Monk'), I did very well. As a celibate monk, I know little of the details of intimacy, but the underlying problems raised by the callers were easily recognised. Soon all the incoming phone calls were directed at me, and I ended up doing most of the work on the two-hour show. But it was the professional sexologist who received the fat cheque. All I got, being a monk who can't receive money, was one chocolate bar. Buddhist wisdom solved the underlying problem again. You can't eat a cheque, and that chocolate bar was delicious. Problem solved, mmm!

At another talkback show on radio, a caller presented me with the following question: 'I'm married. I'm having an affair with another woman, and my wife doesn't know. Is this alright?'

How would you answer?

'If it was alright,' I replied, 'you wouldn't be ringing me to ask.'

Many people ask such questions knowing that what they are doing is wrong, but in the hope that some 'expert' will convince them it is right. Deep inside, most people know what's right and wrong—only some don't listen carefully.

Unwise listening

The phone rang one evening at our Buddhist centre. 'Is Ajahn Brahm there?' demanded the angry caller. 'I'm sorry,' replied the devout Asian woman who picked up the phone. 'He's resting in his room. Please call back in thirty minutes.'

'Grr! He'll be dead in thirty minutes,' growled the caller and then he hung up.

Twenty minutes later, when I came out of my room, the elderly Asian woman was still sitting white-faced and trembling. Others were around her trying to find out what was wrong, but she was too shocked to speak. But when I coaxed her she blurted out, 'Someone's coming to kill you!'

I had been counselling a young Australian man since he was first declared HIV positive. I had taught him meditation and many wisdom strategies to help him cope. Now he was nearing his death. I had visited him only the day before and was expecting a call from his partner at any time. So I soon figured out what the call had meant. It was not me who would be dead in thirty minutes, it was the young man with AIDS.

I rushed to his home and saw him before he died. Fortunately, I also explained the misunderstanding to the terrified Asian woman before she died too, from shock!

How often are what is said and what we hear not the same?

What wisdom is not

A few years ago a number of scandals involving Thai monks appeared in the international press. Monks are bound by their rules to observe celibacy strictly.

In my tradition, to be beyond all suspicion regarding celibacy, monks aren't allowed to have any physical contact with a woman, nor are nuns allowed physical contact with a man. In the scandals that were publicised, some monks had not kept those rules. They were naughty monks. And the press knew that their readers were only interested in naughty monks, not the boring, rule-keeping ones.

At the time of these events, I thought it was high time I made my own confession. So one Friday evening in our temple in Perth, before an audience of some three hundred people, some of them long-standing supporters, I summoned up courage and told them the truth.

'I have a confession to make,' I began. 'This is not easy. Some years ago …' I hesitated.

'Some years ago,' I managed to continue, 'I spent some of the happiest hours of my life …' I had to pause again. 'I spent some of the happiest hours of my life … in the loving arms of another man's wife.' I'd said it. I'd confessed.

'We hugged. We caressed. We kissed.' I finished. Then I hung my head and stared at the carpet.

I could hear the sound of air suddenly drawn in through the mouth in shock. Hands were covering gaping mouths. I heard a few whispers, 'Oh no! Not Ajahn Brahm.' I pictured many long-standing supporters heading for the door, never to return. Even lay Buddhists didn't go with other men's wives—that's adultery. I raised my head, looked at my audience confidently, and smiled.

'That woman,' I explained before anyone was out of the door. 'That woman was my mother. When I was a baby.' My audience exploded in laughter, and relief.

'Well it was true!' I shouted through the microphone above the howling. 'She was another man's wife, my Dad's. We hugged, we caressed, and we kissed. They were some of the happiest hours of my life.'

When my audience had wiped off their tears and stopped giggling, I pointed out that nearly all of them had judged me, mistakenly. Even though they had heard the words from my own mouth, and their meaning seemed so clear, they had leapt to the wrong conclusion. Fortunately, or rather because it was carefully planned, I was able to point out their error. 'How many times,' I asked of them, 'are we not so fortunate, and jump to conclusions, on evidence that seems so certain, only to be wrong, disastrously wrong?' Judging absolutely—'This is right, all else is wrong'—is not wisdom.

The danger of an open mouth

Our politicians have a reputation for being open, especially in the area between their nose and their chin. Such has been the tradition for many a century, as the following proverb from the Buddhist Jataka tales shows.

A King, many centuries ago, was exasperated by one of his ministers. Whenever a matter for discussion came up at court, this minister would interrupt and begin a monologue, which always seemed to go on forever. No one, not even the King, could get a word in. Furthermore, what the minister had to say was even more uninteresting than the inside of a ping-pong ball.

After yet another unproductive session, the King sought peace in his garden away from the frustration of court politics. In the public part of his garden, he spotted a small group of children laughing excitedly as they gathered around a middle-aged, disabled man who was sitting on the ground. The children gave the man a few coins, pointed to a small, leafy tree and asked him for a chicken. The man took out a bag of small stones and a peashooter and began to fire the stones at the tree.

He stripped leaf after leaf off the small tree with rapid-fire shots from his peashooter. In an incredibly short time, and with flawless accuracy, he shaped the tree like a rooster. The children gave him some more money, pointed to a large bush and asked for an elephant. The disabled marksman soon sculpted the bush with his peashooter into the form of an elephant. As the children applauded, the King had an idea.

The King went up to the disabled man and offered to make him rich beyond his wildest dreams, if only he would help with an irritating little problem. The King whispered something into the man's ear. The man nodded in agreement and the King smiled for the first time in weeks.

The following morning, court began as usual. Nobody took much notice of the new curtain along one of the walls. The government was to discuss another increase in taxes. No sooner had the King announced the agenda, than the manic-mouthed minister began his harangue. As he opened his mouth, he felt something small and soft hit the back of his throat and fall down into his stomach. He carried on speaking. A few seconds later, something small and soft entered his mouth again. He gulped it down mid-sentence and continued his speech. Again and again he had to swallow during his speech, but such irritations were not going to stop what he had to say. After half an hour of determined lecturing, gulping down whatever it was every few seconds, he was feeling very, very queasy. But such was his stubbornness that he would not stop his oratory. After another few minutes, his face was a sickly green colour, his stomach was turning with nausea, and he finally had to stop speaking. With one hand holding his sickly stomach and another pressed hard against his mouth to stop something nasty coming out, he desperately sought the nearest washroom.

The delighted King went over to the curtain and drew it back to reveal the disabled man, who had been hiding behind the curtain with his peashooter and a bag of ammunition. The King shook helplessly with laughter as he saw the huge and now almost empty bag of ammunition, chicken shit pellets, that had been projected with devastating accuracy into that poor minister's gullet!

That minister did not return to the court for several weeks. It was remarkable how much business was completed during his absence. Then when he did return, he would hardly say a word. And when he did speak, he would always raise his right hand in front of his mouth.[8]

Perhaps, in our parliaments of today, the presence of such a sharp shooter would get more business done!

The talkative tortoise

Maybe we should learn silence early in our life: it might help us avoid much of the trouble later on. I tell the following story to visiting children on the vital importance of keeping quiet.

In a lake in the mountains a long time ago, there lived a talkative tortoise. Whenever he met any of the animals that shared his waterside home, he would talk to them so much and for so long, without any pauses, that his listeners became bored, then bothered, then annoyed. They often wondered how talkative tortoise was able to talk so long without taking a breath. They thought he must have been breathing through his ears, since he never used them for listening. He was such a torturing talkative tortoise that rabbits would suddenly dive into their holes, birds would fly to the tops of the trees, and fish would hide behind rocks whenever they saw talkative tortoise approaching. They knew that they would be stuck there for hours if talkative tortoise started talking to them. Talkative tortoise was actually quite lonely.

Every year in the summer, a pair of magnificent white swans would come on vacation to the mountain lake. They were kind, because they let talkative tortoise talk to them as much as he liked. Or perhaps they knew they would only be visiting for a couple of months. Talkative tortoise adored the company of the swans. He would talk to them until the stars ran out of twinkle, and the swans would always listen patiently.

When summer was fading and the days became cold, the swans prepared to go home. Talkative tortoise began to cry. He hated the cold, and the loss of his friends.

'If only I could go with you,' he sighed. 'Sometimes, when the snow covers the slopes and my lake ices over, I feel so cold and alone. We tortoises cannot fly. And if I were to walk, by the time I got even a little way, it would be time to come back. Tortoises walk slowly.'

The compassionate swans were touched by the sadness in talkative tortoise. So they made him an offer.

'Dear tortoise, don't cry. We can take you with us, if you can keep only one promise.'

'Yes! Yes! I promise!' said talkative tortoise excitedly, though he did not know what he had to promise yet. 'We tortoises always keep our promises. In fact, I remember promising to rabbit to try and be quiet only a few days ago after I told him all about the different types of tortoise shells and ...'

One hour later, when talkative tortoise stopped talking and the swans could speak again, they said, 'Tortoise, you must promise to keep your mouth shut.'

'Easy!' said talkative tortoise. 'In fact, we tortoises are well known for keeping our mouths shut. We hardly ever speak at all. I was explaining just this to a fish just the other day ...'

One more hour later, when talkative tortoise paused again, the swans told talkative tortoise to bite on to the middle of a long stick and make sure he kept his mouth shut.

Then one swan took one end of the stick into her beak, and the second swan closed his beak onto the other end of the stick. They flapped their wings and ... nothing happened! Talkative tortoise was too heavy. People who talk a lot tend to eat a lot. And talkative tortoise was so fat that sometimes he couldn't even squeeze into his own shell. The swans chose a lighter stick. Then, with the swans biting either end of the stick, and talkative tortoise biting the middle, the two swans flapped their wings as hard as any swans have ever flapped before and rose up into the air. With the swans rose the stick. And with the stick rose the tortoise.

This was the first time, in the history of our world, that a tortoise ever flew.

Higher and higher they soared. Talkative tortoise's lake grew smaller and smaller. Even the huge mountains now seemed tiny in the distance. He was seeing amazing sights that no other tortoise had ever seen before. He was carefully trying to remember it all, to tell his friends, of course, when he got back home.

Over the mountains they flew and then down to the plains. All was going well until, about half past three in the afternoon, they passed over a school where the children had just come out. A small boy happened to look up. What do you think he saw? A flying tortoise!

'Hey!' he shouted to his friends. 'Look at that stupid tortoise, flying!'

The tortoise couldn't stop himself.

'Who are you calling ... oops! ... stuuu ... piiii ... d!' 'SPLAT!' went talkative tortoise as he crashed to the ground. And that was the last sound he made.[9]

Talkative tortoise died because he couldn't keep his mouth shut when it really mattered.

So if you don't learn how to keep quiet at the proper times, then when it is very important you will not be able to keep your mouth shut. You might end up as a hamburger patty, like the talkative tortoise.

Free speech

I am surprised that speech is still free in our modern market driven economies. It must only be a matter of time before some cash-strapped government regards words as another commodity and puts a tax on speech.

On reflection, it might not be such a bad idea. Silence would once again become golden. Phone lines would no longer be tied up by teenagers and the queues at supermarket checkouts would flow freely. Marriages would last longer as young couples simply couldn't afford the cost of an argument. And it would be comforting to consider that certain of your acquaintances would be contributing enough public revenue to supply free hearing aids to those they have deafened over the years. It would shift the tax burden from the hard workers onto the hard talkers. Of course, the most generous contributors to such a splendid tax scheme would be the politicians themselves. The more they argue in parliament, the more money would be raised for our hospitals and schools. How satisfying a thought.

Lastly, for those who might think such a tax scheme impractical, who could afford to argue vigorously against it?

The mind and reality

The exorcist

The following is a true story of the supernatural in Thailand, of the supernatural wisdom of the amazing Ajahn Chah.

The headman of a nearby village, with one of his assistants, walked in hurriedly to see Ajahn Chah under his hut, where he received guests. One of the village women had become possessed by a violent and evil spirit the previous evening. They could not help her, so they were bringing her to the great monk. As they spoke with Ajahn Chah, screaming could be heard not far away.

Ajahn Chah immediately ordered two novices to start a fire and boil up some water; then he told two other novices to dig a big hole close to his hut. None of the novices knew why.

Four strong village men, tough northeastern rice-farmers, were hardly able to contain the writhing woman. As they dragged her through one of the holiest of monasteries; she was screaming obscenities.

Ajahn Chah saw her and barked at the novices: 'Dig faster! Get that water boiling! We'll need a big hole and lots of boiling water.' Not even the monks and villagers under Ajahn Chah's hut could figure out what he was up to. As they pulled the screaming woman under Ajahn Chah's hut she was literally foaming at the mouth. Her blood-red eyes were stretched wide with her madness. And her face assumed crazy contortions as she hurled crudity after obscenity at Ajahn Chah. More men joined in to hold down the spitting woman.

'Is the hole dug yet? Quick! Is the water boiled? Faster!' Ajahn Chah shouted above the yells of the woman. 'We have to throw her in the hole. Pour the boiling water all over her.

Then bury her. That's the only way to get rid of this evil spirit. Dig Faster! More boiling water!'

We had learned from experience that no one could be sure what Ajahn Chah might do. He was uncertainty in the form of a monk. The villagers certainly thought he was about to throw the possessed woman into the hole, scald her all over with boiling water and bury her. And they would let him. She must have thought so too, because she started to grow calm. Before the hole was completed, and before the water was boiled, she was sitting calmly in the peace of exhaustion in front of Ajahn Chah, gracefully receiving a blessing before they gently led her home. Brilliant.

Ajahn Chah knew that, possessed or just crazy, there is something powerful inside each one of us called self preservation. He skilfully, and very dramatically, pressed that button in her, and let the fear of pain and death exorcise the demon possessing her.

That's wisdom: intuitive, unplanned, unrepeatable.

The biggest thing in the world

The daughter of a friend from my college days was in her first year at primary school. Her teacher asked the large class of five-year-olds, 'What is the biggest thing in the world?'

'My daddy,' said one small girl.

'An elephant,' answered a young boy who had recently been to the zoo.

'A mountain,' replied another.

My friend's young child said, 'My eye is the biggest thing in the world.'

The class went quiet as they all tried to understand the little girl's answer. 'What do you mean?' asked her teacher, equally perplexed.

'Well,' began the miniature philosopher, 'My eye can see her daddy, and it can see an elephant. It can also see a mountain and many other things as well. Since all this can fit into my eye, my eye must be the biggest thing in the world!'

Wisdom is not learning, but seeing clearly what can never be taught.

With much respect to my friend's young daughter, I would extend her insight a little further. It is not your eye but your mind that is the biggest thing in the world.

Your mind can see all that your eye can see, and it can see more that is supplied through your imagination. It can also know sounds, which your eye can never see, and know touch, both real and made of dream stuff. Your mind can also know what lies outside your five senses. Because everything that can be known can fit into your mind, your mind must be the biggest thing in the world. The mind contains all.

Searching for the mind

Many scientists and their supporters assert that the mind is merely a by-product of the brain, so in question time after my talks I am often asked: 'Does the mind exist? If so, where? Is it in the body? Or is it outside? Or is it everywhere and all over? Where is the mind?'

To answer this question, I conduct a simple demonstration. I ask my audience: 'If you are happy right now, raise your right hand please. If you are unhappy, even a little, please raise your left hand.' Most people raise their right hand, some truly, the rest out of pride.

'Now,' I continue, 'those who are happy, please point to that happiness with your right index finger. Those who are unhappy, please point to that unhappiness with your left index finger. Locate it for me.'

My audience begin to wave their fingers pointlessly up and down. Then they glance around at their neighbours in similar confusion. When they get the message, they laugh.

Happiness is real. Unhappiness is true. There is no doubt that these things exist. But you cannot locate these realities anywhere in your body, anywhere outside of your body, or anywhere at all.

This is because happiness and unhappiness are part of the territory exclusive to the mind. They belong to the mind, like flowers and weeds belong to the garden. The fact that flowers and weeds exist proves that a garden exists. In just the same way, the fact that happiness and unhappiness exist proves that the mind exists.

The discovery that you cannot point to happiness or unhappiness shows that you cannot locate the mind in three-dimensional space. Indeed, remembering that the mind is the biggest thing in the world—the mind cannot be within three-dimensional space, but three-dimensional space is within the mind. The mind is the biggest thing in the world, it contains the universe.

Science

I was a scientist before becoming a monk. I explored the Zen-like world of theoretical physics at Cambridge University in England. Science and religion, I have found, hold many things in common, one of which is dogma. A delightfully descriptive saying I remember from my student days was: 'The eminence of a great scientist is measured by the length of time he or she obstructs progress in their field!'

At a recent debate in Australia between science and religion, at which I was a speaker, I took a poignant question from a member of the audience: 'When I look through a telescope at the beauty of the stars,' said the devout Catholic woman, 'I always feel that my religion is threatened.'

'Madam, when a scientist looks down the other end of a telescope, from the big end to the small end,' I replied, 'to gaze upon the one who is looking, then science is threatened!'

The science of silence

Perhaps it is better to stop arguing altogether. A famous Eastern proverb goes:

He who knows, doesn't say; He who says, doesn't know.

This might sound profound until you work out that whoever said it, therefore didn't know!

Blind faith

When we get old our eyesight fades, our hearing goes, our hair falls out, our false teeth go in, our legs become weak and our hands sometimes shake. But the one part of our anatomy that seems to get ever stronger with each passing year is our talkative mouth. This is why the most verbose of our citizens may qualify as politicians only in their later years.

A King many centuries ago had trouble with his ministers. They would argue so much that almost nothing was decided. The ministers, following the most ancient of political traditions, each claimed that they alone were right and everyone else was wrong. However, when the resourceful King organised a special public festival, they all agreed to take the day off.

The festival was a spectacular affair held in the large stadium. There was singing and dancing, acrobatics, clowns, music and much else. Then for the finale in front of the huge crowd, with the ministers occupying the best seats of course, the King himself led his royal elephant into the centre of the arena. Following the elephant came seven blind men, known in the city to have been blind since birth.

The King took the hand of the first blind man, helped him feel the elephant's trunk and told him that this is an elephant. He then helped the second blind man feel the elephant's tusk, the third one its ears, the fourth the head, the fifth the torso, the sixth the legs, and the seventh the tail, telling each one that this was an elephant. Then he returned to the first blind man and asked him to say in a loud voice what an elephant was.

'In my considered and expert opinion,' said the first blind man, feeling the trunk, 'I state with utmost certainty that an "elephant" is a species of snake, genus *Python asiaticus*.'

'What twittering twaddle!' exclaimed the second blind man, feeling a tusk. 'An "elephant" is much too solid to be a snake. In actual fact, and I am never wrong, it is a farmer's plough.'

'Don't be ridiculous!' jeered the third blind man, feeling an ear. 'An "elephant" is a palm-leaf fan.'

'You incompetent idiots!' laughed the fourth blind man, feeling the head. 'An "elephant" is obviously a large water jar.'

'Impossible! Absolutely impossible!' ranted the fifth blind man, feeling the torso. 'An "elephant" is a huge rock.'

'Bulldust!' shouted the sixth blind man, feeling a leg. 'An "elephant" is a tree trunk.'

'What a bunch of twerps!' sneered the last blind man, feeling the tail. 'I'll tell you what an "elephant" really is. It is a kind of fly whisk. I know, I can feel it!'

'Rubbish! It's a snake.' 'Can't be! It's a jar.' 'No way! It's a …' And the blind men started arguing so heatedly, and all at the same time, that the words melted together in one loud and long yell. As the insults flew, so did the fists. Though the blind men weren't quite sure who they were hitting, it didn't seem that important in the fury of the fracas. They were fighting for principle, for integrity, for truth. Their own individual truth, that was.

While the King's soldiers were separating the blind and bruised brawlers, the crowd in the stadium was mocking the silent, shamefaced ministers. Everyone who was there had well understood the point of the King's object lesson.[10]

Each one of us can know only a part of the whole that constitutes truth. When we hold on to our limited knowledge as absolute truth, we are like one of the blind men feeling a part of the elephant and inferring that their own partial experience is the truth, all else being wrong.

Instead of blind faith, we can have dialogue. Imagine the result if the seven blind men, instead of opposing their data, had combined their experience. They would have concluded that an 'elephant' is something like a huge rock standing on four stout tree trunks. On the back of the rock is a flywhisk, on the front a large water jar. At the sides of the jar are two palm-leaf fans, with two ploughs towards the bottom and a long python in the middle! That would not be such a bad description of an elephant, for one who will never see one.

Values and the spiritual life

The most beautiful sound

An uneducated old man was visiting a city for the first time in his life. He had grown up in a remote mountain village, worked hard raising his children, and was now enjoying his first visit to his children's modern homes.

One day, while being shown around the city, the old man heard a sound that stung his ears. He had never heard such an awful noise in his quiet mountain village and he insisted on finding its cause. Following the grating sound back to its source, he came to a room in the back of a house where a small boy was practising on a violin.

'SCREECH! SCRAPE!' came the discordant notes from the groaning violin.

When he was told by his son that it was called a 'violin', he decided he never wanted to hear such a horrible thing again.

The next day, in a different part of the city, the old man heard a sound, which seemed to caress his aged ears. He had never heard such an enchanting melody in his mountain valley, so he demanded to find its cause. Following the delightful sound back to its source, he came to a room in the front of a house where an old lady, a maestro, was performing a sonata on a violin.

At once, the old man realised his mistake. The terrible sound that he had heard the previous day was not the fault of the violin, nor even of the boy. It was just that the young man had yet to learn his instrument well.

With a wisdom reserved for the simple folk, the old man thought it was the same with religion. When we come across a religious enthusiast causing such strife with his beliefs, it is incorrect to blame the religion. It is just that the novice has yet to learn his religion well. When we come across a saint, a maestro of her religion, it is such a sweet encounter that it inspires us for many years, whatever their beliefs.

But that was not the end of the story.

The third day, in a different part of the city, the old man heard another sound that surpassed in its beauty and purity even that of the maestro on her violin. What do you think that sound was?

It was a sound more beautiful than the cascade of the mountain stream in spring, than the autumn wind through the forest groves, or than the mountain birds singing after a heavy rain. It was even more beautiful than the silence in the mountain hollows on a still winter's night. What was that sound that moved the old man's heart more powerfully than anything before?

It was a large orchestra playing a symphony.

The reason that it was, for the old man, the most beautiful sound in the world was, firstly, that every member of that orchestra was a maestro of their own instrument; and secondly, that they had further learned how to play together in harmony.

'May it be the same with religion,' the old man thought. 'Let each one of us learn through the lessons of life the soft heart of our beliefs. Let us each be a maestro of the love within our religion. Then, having learned our religion well, let us go further and learn how to play, like members of an orchestra, with other religions in harmony together!'

That would be the most beautiful sound.

What's in a name?

When one becomes a Buddhist monk in our tradition, one receives a new name. My monk's name is 'Brahmavamso', which, being so long, I usually shorten to 'Brahm'. Everyone calls me by that name now, except for my Mum. She still calls me Peter, and I defend her right to do so.

Once, during a phone call inviting me to an interfaith ceremony, I was asked to spell my name. I answered:

B—for Buddhist
R—for Roman Catholic
A—for Anglican
H—for Hindu
M—for Muslim

I received such a positive response that I usually spell my name that way now, and also that's what it means.

Pyramid power

In the summer of 1969, just after my eighteenth birthday, I was enjoying my first experience of tropical jungles. I was travelling in the Yucatán peninsula of Guatemala, heading for the recently discovered pyramids of the vanished Mayan civilisation.

In those days, travel was difficult. It took me three or four days to cover the few hundred kilometres from Guatemala City to the ruined temple complex known as Tical. I travelled up narrow rainforest rivers on oil-soaked fishing boats, down winding dirt roads balanced precariously on top of heavily loaded trucks, and through small jungle paths on rattling, ramshackle rickshaws. It was a region remote, poor and pristine.

When I finally arrived at the extensive complex of abandoned temples and ancient pyramids, I had neither guide nor guidebook to tell me the meaning of those impressive stone monuments pointing to the sky. Nobody was around. So I started climbing one of the tall pyramids.

On reaching the top, the meaning and spiritual purpose of these pyramids became suddenly clear to me.

For the previous three days, I had been travelling exclusively through jungle. The roads, paths and rivers were like tunnels through the dense greenery. Jungle quickly made a ceiling above any new thoroughfare. I hadn't seen the horizon for many days. Indeed, I hadn't seen far distances at all. I was in jungle.

On top of that pyramid, I was above the tangle of the jungle. Not only could I see where I was in the map-like panorama laid out before me, but I could now see in all directions, with nothing between infinity and me.

Standing up there, as if on top of the world, I imagined what it might have been like for young Mayan Indians who had been born in the jungle, raised in the jungle and lived all their life in the jungle. I pictured them in some religious rite of passage being led gently by the hand, by a wise old holy man, up to the summit of a pyramid for the very first time. When they rose above the tree line and beheld their jungle world unfolded and spread out before them, when they gazed beyond the limits of their territory to the horizon and what lies beyond, they would see the great embracing emptiness above and around. Standing on the point of the pyramid, in the doorway between heaven and earth, there would be no person, no thing, no word between them and the infinite in every direction. Their heart would resonate with the striking symbolism of the scene. Truths would flower and send forth the fragrance of knowing. They would understand their place in their home world, and they would have seen the infinite, the freeing emptiness, which embraces it all. Their life would have found its meaning.

We all need to grant ourselves the time and the peace to climb that spiritual pyramid inside each one of us, to rise above and beyond the tangled jungle that is our life, if only for a short time. Then we may see for ourself our place among things, the overview of our life journey, and gaze unimpeded at the infinite in every direction.

Precious stones

At a famous US business school some years ago, a professor delivered an extraordinary lecture on social economics to his graduate class. Without explaining what he was doing, the professor carefully placed a glass jar on his desk. Then, in view of his students, he brought out a bag full of stones and placed them one by one in the jar, until no more would go in. He asked his students, 'Is the jar full?'

'Yes,' they replied.

The professor smiled. From beneath the desk, the professor produced a second bag, this one full of gravel. He then managed to shake the smaller stones into the spaces between the bigger stones in the jar. A second time, he asked the students, 'Is the jar full?'

'No,' they answered. They were on to him by now.

They were correct, of course, for the professor produced a bag of fine sand. He managed to coax much of the sand into the spaces between the stones and the gravel within the jar. Again he asked, 'Is the jar full?'

'Probably not, Sir, knowing you,' the students replied. Smiling at their answer, the professor brought out a small jug of water, which he poured into the jar full of stones, gravel and sand. When no more water would fit in the jar, he put down the jug and looked at his class.

'So, what does this teach you?' he asked his students. 'That no matter how busy your schedule,' offered one of the students, 'you can always fit something more in!' It was a famous business school, after all.

'No!' thundered the professor emphatically. 'What it shows is that if you want to get the big stones in, you have to put them in first.'

It was a lesson in priorities.

So what are the 'big stones' in your 'jar'? What is most important to fit in to your life? Please ensure that you schedule in the 'precious stones' first, or you'll never get around to them, to fit them into your day.

Then I'll be happy

Perhaps the most precious of stones to have in our 'jar' early, as in the previous story, is inner happiness. When we have no happiness inside us, we have no happiness to give to others. So why do so many of us give such low priority to happiness, postponing it to the very end? (Or even after the very end, as the following story will show.)

When I was fourteen years old, I was studying for my O-level examinations in a high school in London. My parents and teachers advised me to stop playing soccer in the evenings and weekends—to stay at home instead giving the time to my homework. They explained how important the O-level exams were and that if I did well, then I'd be happy.

I followed their advice and did very well. But it didn't make me that happy, because my success meant that now I must study even harder, for another two years, for the A-level exams. My parents and teachers advised me to stop going out in the evenings and weekends, to stop chasing girls now rather than chasing a football, and to stay at home instead and study. They told me how important the A-level exams were and that if I did well, then I'd be happy.

Once again, I followed their advice and did very well. Once again, it didn't make me very happy. Because now I had to study hardest of all, for three more long years, for a degree at a university. My mother and teachers (my father was now dead) advised me to steer clear of the bars and parties in college, but instead to work hard and long at my studies. They told me how important a university degree was, and that if I did well, then I'd be happy.

At this point, I started to become suspicious.

I saw some of my older friends who had worked very hard and got their degree. Now they were working even harder in their first job. They were working extremely hard to save up enough money to buy something important, say, a car. They told me, 'When I have enough money to buy a car, then I'll be happy.'

When they had enough funds and had bought their first car, they still weren't happy. Now they were working hard to buy something else, and then they'd be happy. Or they were struggling in the turmoil of romance, looking for a partner in life. They told me, 'When I get married and settle down, then I'll be happy.'

Once married, they still weren't happy. They had to work even harder, even taking extra jobs, to save up enough money for a deposit on an apartment, or even a small house. They told me, 'When we have bought our own house, then we'll be happy.'

Unfortunately, paying off the monthly instalment for the house loan meant that they still weren't very happy. Moreover, they would now start a family. They would have children to wake them up at night, swallow up all their spare money and increase their worries in quantum leaps and bounds. Now it would be another twenty years before they could do what they wanted. So they told me, 'When the kids are grown up, have left home and settled, then we'll be happy.'

By the time the kids had left home, most of the parents were staring at retirement. So they continued to postpone their happiness, working hard to save for their old age. They told me, 'When I retire, then I'll be happy.'

Even before they retired, and certainly after, they started becoming religious and going to church. Have you ever noticed how many old people occupy the pews in a church? I asked them why they were now going to church. They told me, 'Because, when I die, then I'll be happy!'

For those who believe that 'When I get this, then I'll be happy', their happiness will be just a dream in the future. It will be like a rainbow one or two steps ahead, but forever just out of reach. They will never in their life, or after, realise happiness.

The Mexican fisherman

In a quiet Mexican fishing village, an American on vacation was watching a local fisherman unload his morning catch. The American, a successful professor at a prestigious US business school, couldn't resist giving the Mexican fisherman a little bit of free advice.

'Hey!' began the American. 'Why are you finishing so early?'

'Since I have caught enough fish, Señor,' replied the genial Mexican, 'enough to feed my family and a little extra to sell. Now I will take some lunch with my wife and, after a little siesta in the afternoon, I will play with my children. Then, after dinner, I will go to the cantina, drink a little tequila and play some guitar with my friends. It is enough for me, Señor.'

'Listen to me, my friend,' said the business professor. 'If you stay out at sea until late afternoon, you will easily catch twice as much fish. You can sell the extra, save up the money, and in six months, maybe nine, you'll be able to buy a bigger and better boat and hire some crew. Then you'll be able to catch four times as many fish. Think of the extra money you will make! In another year or two, you will have the capital to buy a second fishing boat and hire another crew. If you follow this business plan, in six or seven years you will be the proud owner of a large fishing fleet. Just imagine that! Then you should move your head office to Mexico City, or even to LA. After only three or four years in LA, you float your company on the stock market giving yourself, as CEO, a generous salary package with substantial share options. In a few more years—listen to this!—you initiate a company share buy-back scheme, which will make you a multi-millionaire! Guaranteed! I'm a well-known professor at a US business school. I know these things.'

The Mexican fisherman listened thoughtfully at what the animated American had to say. When the professor had finished, the Mexican asked him, 'But, Señor Professor, what will I do with so many millions of dollars?'

Surprisingly, the American professor hadn't thought the business plan through that far. So he quickly figured out what a person would do with millions of dollars.

'Amigo! With all that dough, you can retire. Yeah! Retire for life. You can buy a little villa in a picturesque fishing village like this one, and purchase a small boat for going fishing in the morning. You can have lunch with your wife every day, and a siesta afterwards with nothing to worry you. In the afternoon you can spend quality time with your kids and, after dinner in the evening, play guitar with your friends in the cantina, drinking tequila. Yeah, with all that money, my friend, you can retire and take it easy.'

'But, Señor Professor, I do all that already.'

Why do we believe that we have to work so hard and get rich first, before we can find contentment?

When all my wishes were fulfilled

In my tradition, monks aren't allowed to accept, own or handle any money, whatever its kind. We are so poor that we mess up government statistics.

We live frugally on the unsolicited, simple gifts from our lay supporters. However, infrequently we may be offered something special.

I had helped a Thai man with a personal problem. Out of gratitude, he said to me: 'Sir, I would like to give you something for your personal use. What can I get you for the amount of five hundred baht?' It was usual to quote the amount when making such an offering, to avoid any misunderstanding. Since I couldn't think what I wanted straight away and he was in a hurry, we agreed that I could tell him the next day when he returned.

Before this occurred, I was a happy little monk. Now I started to contemplate what I wanted. I made a list. The list grew. Soon, five hundred baht wasn't enough. But it was so difficult to take anything off the list. Wants had appeared out of nowhere and solidified into absolute necessities. And the list kept growing. Now, five thousand baht wasn't sufficient!

Seeing what was happening, I threw my wish list away. The next day, I told my benefactor to give the five hundred baht to the monastery building fund or to some other good cause. I didn't want it. What I wanted most of all was to regain the rare contentment I had had the day before. When I had no money, nor the means to get anything, that was the time when all my wishes were fulfilled.

Wanting has no end to it. Even one billion baht isn't enough, nor one billion dollars. But freedom from wanting has an end. It is when you want for nothing. Contentment is the only time you have enough.

Freedom and humility

Two kinds of freedom

There are two kinds of freedom to be found in our world: the freedom of desires, and the freedom from desires.

Our modern Western culture only recognises the first of these, freedom of desires. It then worships such a freedom by enshrining it at the forefront of national constitutions and bills of human rights. One can say that the underlying creed of most Western democracies is to protect their people's freedom to realise their desires, as far as this is possible. It is remarkable that in such countries people do not feel very free.

The second kind of freedom, freedom from desires, is celebrated only in some religious communities. It celebrates contentment, peace that is free from desires. It is remarkable that in such abstemious communities like my monastery, people feel free.

Which type of freedom would you like?

Two highly attained Thai monks had been invited to a lay supporter's home to take their morning meal. In the reception room where they were waiting, there was a decorative fish tank stocked with many species. The junior of the monks complained that it was contrary to the Buddhist principle of compassion to keep fish in an aquarium. It was like putting them in a prison. What had the fish done to deserve being incarcerated in a glass-walled jail? They should be free to swim in the rivers and lakes, going wherever they pleased. The second monk disagreed. It was true, he conceded, that those fish were not free to follow their desires, but living in a fish tank gave them freedom from so many dangers. Then he listed their freedoms.

1 Have you ever seen a fisherman drop a line into the aquarium in someone's house? No! So the first freedom for fish in a tank is freedom from the danger of fishermen.

Imagine what it must be like for a fish in the wild. When they see a succulent worm or a juicy fat fly they can never be sure whether it is safe to eat or not. They have, no doubt, seen many of their friends and relations tuck in to a delicious-looking worm, and then suddenly disappear upwards out of their life forever. For a fish in the wild, eating is fraught with danger and often ends in tragedy. Dinner is traumatic. All fish must suffer chronic indigestion due to anxiety complexes over every meal, and the paranoid ones would surely starve to death. Fish in the wild are probably psychotic. But fish in a tank are free from this danger.

2 Fish in the wild also have to worry about bigger fish eating them. In some decadent rivers these days, it is no longer safe to go up a dark creek at night! However, no owner would place fish in their tank that are given to eating one another. So fish in a tank are free from the danger of cannibal fish.

3 In the cycles of nature, fish in the wild sometimes go without food. But for fish in a tank, it must be like living next door to a restaurant. Two times a day, a well-balanced meal is delivered to their door, more convenient even than a pizza home delivery, since they don't have to pay. So fish in a tank are also free from the danger of hunger.

4 As the seasons change, rivers and lakes are subject to temperature extremes. They get so cold in winter, they

may be covered with ice. In summer, they may be too warm for fish, sometimes even drying up. But the fish in a tank have the equivalent of reverse-cycle air-conditioning. The water temperature in the tank is kept constant and comfortable, throughout the day and all year. So fish in a tank are free from the danger of heat and cold.

5 In the wild, when fish get ill, there is no one to treat them. But fish in a tank have free medical insurance. Their owner will bring a fish doctor on a house call whenever there's an ailment; they don't even need to go to a clinic. So fish in a tank are free from the danger of no health cover.

The second monk, the elder of the two, summed up his position. There are many advantages to being a fish in an aquarium, he said. True, they are not free to follow their desires and swim here and there, but they are free from so many dangers and discomforts.

The elder monk went on to explain that it is the same with people who live a virtuous life. True, they are not free to follow their desires and indulge here and there, but they are free from so many dangers and discomforts.

Which type of freedom would you like?

The Free World

For several weeks, one of my fellow monks had been teaching meditation in a new maximum-security prison close to Perth. The small group of prisoners had come to know and respect the monk well. At the end of one session, they began to ask him about his routine in a Buddhist monastery.

'We have to get up a 4.00 a.m. every morning,' he began. 'Sometimes it is very cold because our small rooms don't have heaters. We eat only one meal a day, all mixed together in the one bowl. In the afternoon and at night-time we can eat nothing at all. There is no sex or alcohol, of course. Nor do we have television, radio or music. We never watch movies, nor can we play sport. We talk little, work hard and spend our free time sitting cross-legged watching our breath. We sleep on the floor.'

The inmates were stunned at the spartan austerity of our monastic life. It made their high-security prison appear like a five-star hotel in comparison. In fact, one of the prisoners was so moved with sympathy for the plight of their monk friend that he forgot where he was and said: 'That's terrible living in your monastery. Why don't you come in here and stay with us?'

The monk told me that everyone in the room cracked up with laughter. So did I when he related the incident. Then I began to contemplate it deeply.

It is true that my monastery is far more ascetic than the severest of prisons for society's felons, yet many come to stay of their free will, and are happy here. Whereas many want to escape from the well-appointed prison, and are unhappy there. Why?

It is because, in my monastery, the inmates want to be there; in a prison, the inmates don't want to be there. That is the difference.

Any place you don't want to be, no matter how comfortable, is a prison for you. This is the real meaning of the word 'prison'—any situation where you don't want to be. If you are in a job where you don't want to be, then you are in a prison. If you are in a relationship where you don't want to be, you are also in a prison. If you are in a sick and painful body where you don't want to be, then that too is a prison for you. A prison is any situation where you don't want to be.

So how do you escape from the many prisons of life? Easy. Just change your perception of your situation into 'wanting to be there'. Even in San Quentin, or the next best thing—my monastery—when you want to be there, then it is no longer a prison for you. By changing your perception of your job, relationship or sick body, and by accepting the situation rather than not wanting it, then it no longer feels like a prison. When you are content to be here, then you are free.

Freedom is being content to be where you are. Prison is wanting to be somewhere else. The Free World is the world experienced by one who is content. The real freedom is freedom from desire, never freedom of desire.

A dinner with Amnesty International

Considering the harsh conditions of life in my monastery, I am very careful to cultivate good relations with Perth's local chapter of Amnesty International. So when I received an invitation to a dinner hosted by Amnesty International, to celebrate the fiftieth anniversary of the Universal Declaration of Human Rights, I sent them the following reply:

> Dear Julia, Promotions Officer,
>
> Thank you most kindly for your recent letter to me concerning the 50th anniversary of the UDHR dinner on Saturday 30th May. I was very flattered to receive an invitation to attend the function.
>
> However, I am a Buddhist monk of the Theravada School, which tradition keeps strictly to a very austere Rule. Unfortunately, this Rule forbids me from eating during the period beginning at noon until the dawn of the next day and so, alas, dinner is out! Alcohol is also a

no-no, and this includes wine. Should I accept your invitation, then, I would be obliged to sit with an empty plate alongside an empty glass all the while watching those around me joyfully devouring what I am sure would be a most sumptuous repast. This would be a form of torture for me which, as Amnesty International, you could never condone!

Moreover, as a Buddhist monk of this tradition, I may neither receive nor possess any money. I remain happily so far below the poverty line that I mess up so many government statistics! So I have no means of paying for the dinner, which I may not eat anyway.

I was going to continue with the problem a monk such as me encounters with the proper dress codes for such a function but I believe I have said enough. I send my apologies that I am unable to attend the dinner.

Yours in happy poverty,

Brahm

The dress code of a monk

Monks of my tradition wear brown robes, and that's all we have. A few years ago, I had to go into an Australian hospital for a few days. On admission, I was asked if I had brought my pyjamas. I said that monks don't wear pyjamas; it is either these robes or nothing! So they let me wear my robes.

The problem is that the monk's dress looks like a dress.

One Sunday afternoon in a suburb of Perth, I was loading our monastery van with supplies for our building work. A thirteen-year-old Aussie girl came out from a nearby house to speak to me. She had never seen a Buddhist monk before.

Standing before me with her hands on her hips, she looked me up and down with utter contempt. Then she began to scold me in a voice full of disgust: 'You're dressed like a girl! That's sick! Yuk!'

She was so over-the-top that I couldn't help laughing. I also remembered my teacher, Ajahn Chah, advising his disciples how to respond when they receive abuse: 'If someone calls you a dog, don't get angry. Instead, just look at your bottom. If you can't see a tail there, then it means you're not a dog. End of problem.'

Sometimes I get compliments for wearing my robes in public. On one occasion, though, it gave me the shivers.

I had business in the city. My driver (monks aren't allowed to drive) had parked our monastery van in a multi-storeyed car park. He announced that he was desperate to go to the toilet, but because he thought that the car park toilets were dirty, he wanted to use the conveniences in a nearby cinema foyer. So, as my driver was attending to nature's business inside, I was waiting outside the cinema, standing in the busy street in my monk's robes.

A young man approached me, smiled sweetly and asked me if I had the time. Monks like me are very innocent. I have lived in a monastery for most of my life. Also, since monks don't wear wristwatches, I had to politely apologise that I did not know the time. He frowned and began to walk away.

When he had only gone a few paces, it suddenly hit me what the guy had meant. 'Have you got the time?' is probably the oldest pick-up line in the book. I was to find out later that I had been left standing in one of the most popular meeting places for gays in Perth!

The gay man turned around to look at me again and said, in his best Marilyn Monroe voice, 'Oooh! But you do look beautiful in those robes!'

I confess to breaking out into a sweat. Just then, my driver emerged from the cinema foyer to rescue me. From that time on, we used the car-park toilets.

Laughing at yourself

One of the best pieces of advice I received as a young schoolteacher was that when you make a mistake and your class starts laughing, then you laugh too. That way, your students are never laughing at you, but with you.

Many years later, as a teaching monk in Perth, I would be invited to high schools to give a lesson on Buddhism. The teenage Western schoolkids would often test me out by trying to embarrass me. Once when I asked for questions from the class, at the end of my description of Buddhist culture, a fourteen-year-old schoolgirl raised her hand and asked: 'Do girls turn you on, then?'

Fortunately, the other girls in the class came to my rescue and scolded the young girl for embarrassing them all. As for me, I laughed and noted the incident down as material for my next talk.

On another occasion, I was walking along a main city street when some schoolgirls approached me. 'Hi!' they said in the most friendly of manners, 'Do you remember us? You came to give a talk at our school a short time ago.'

'I am flattered that you remember me,' I replied.

'We'll never forget you,' said one of the girls, 'How can we ever forget a monk named "Bra"!'

The dog that had the last laugh

My first year as a monk in northeast Thailand coincided with the last year of the Vietnam War. Close to Ajahn Chah's monastery, near the regional city of Ubon, was an American air-force base. Ajahn Chah enjoyed telling us the following true story on how to deal with abuse.

An American GI was travelling from the base into town on a cycle-rickshaw. On the outskirts of town, they passed a roadside bar where some friends of the rickshaw driver were already quite drunk.

'Hey!' they shouted in Thai. 'Where are you taking that dirty dog to?' Then they laughed, pointing at the American soldier.

For a moment, the driver was alarmed. The soldier was a very big man and calling someone a 'dirty dog' meant an inevitable fight. However, the soldier was quietly looking around, enjoying the beautiful scenery. Obviously, he did not understand the Thai language.

The driver, deciding to have some fun at the American's expense, shouted back, 'I'm taking this filthy dog and throwing him in the Moon River to give the smelly mongrel a wash!'

As the driver and his drunken friends laughed, the soldier remained unmoved.

When they reached their destination and the driver put out his hand for the journey's fare, the American soldier quietly began to walk away.

The rickshaw driver excitedly shouted after him in broken but clear English, 'Hey! Sir! You pay me dollars!'

To which the big American soldier calmly turned around and said in the most fluent of Thai, 'Dogs don't have money.'

Abuse and enlightenment

Experienced meditation teachers often have to deal with disciples who claim to be enlightened. One of the time-honoured ways to test if their claims are true is to abuse the disciple so grossly that they end up getting angry. As all Buddhist monks and nuns know, the Buddha clearly stated that one who gets angry is certainly not enlightened.

A young Japanese monk, strenuously intent on nirvana in this very life, was meditating in solitude in a secluded lake-island hermitage near a famous monastery. He wanted to get enlightenment out of the way early on in his life, so he could then attend to other things.

When the monastery attendant arrived in his small row-boat on his weekly visit to deliver supplies, the young monk left a note requesting some expensive parchment, a quill and some fine quality ink. He was soon to complete his third year in solitude and wanted to let his abbot know how well he had done.

The parchment, quill and ink arrived the following week. In the next few days, after much meditating and pondering, the young monk wrote on the fine parchment in the most exquisite of calligraphy the following short poem:

> *"The conscientious young monk,*
> *Meditating three years alone,*
> *Can no longer be moved,*
> *By the four worldly winds."*

Surely, he thought, his wise old abbot would see in these words, and in the care by which they were written, that his disciple was now enlightened. He gently rolled up the parchment, carefully tied it with a ribbon, and then waited for the attendant to deliver it to his teacher. In the days that followed, he imagined his abbot's pleasure at reading the brilliant poem so meticulously inscribed. He could see it being hung in a costly frame in the monastery's main hall. No doubt they would press him to be an abbot now, maybe of a famous city monastery. How nice he felt to have made it at last!

When the attendant next rowed the small boat to the island to deliver the weekly supplies, the young monk was waiting for him. The attendant soon handed the monk a parchment similar to the one he had sent, but tied with a different coloured ribbon. 'From the abbot,' said the attendant tersely.

The monk excitedly tore off the ribbon and unfurled the scroll. As his eyes settled on the parchment, they grew as wide as the moon, and his face went just as white. It was his own parchment, but next to the first line of exquisite calligraphy, the abbot had carelessly scribbled in a red ballpoint pen, 'Fart!' To the right of the second line was another ugly smudge of red ink saying, 'Fart!' The third line had another irreverent 'Fart!' scrawled over it, and so did the fourth line of verse.

This was too much! Not only was the decrepit old abbot so stupid that he couldn't recognise enlightenment when it was in front of his fat nose, but he was so uncouth and uncivilised that he had vandalised a work of art with indecent graffiti. The abbot was behaving like a punk, not a monk. It was an insult to art, to tradition and to truth.

The young monk's eyes narrowed with indignation, his face flushed red with righteous anger, and he snorted as he insisted of the attendant, 'Take me to the abbot! Immediately!'

It was the first time in three years that the young monk had left his island hermitage. In a rage, he stormed into the abbot's office, slammed the parchment on the table and demanded an explanation.

The experienced abbot slowly picked up the parchment, cleared his throat, and read out the poem:

"The conscientious young monk,
Meditating three years alone,
Can no longer be moved,
By the four worldly winds."

Then he put down the parchment, stared at the young monk, and continued. 'Hmm! So, young monk, you are no longer moved by the four worldly winds. Yet four little farts have blown you right across the lake!'

When I became enlightened

In my fourth year as a monk in Thailand, I was practising long and hard in a remote forest monastery in the northeast. Late one night, during an extended spell of walking meditation, my mind grew exceptionally clear. Deep insights came cascading like a mountain waterfall. I was easily understanding profound mysteries that I had never fathomed before. Then the Big One came. It blew me away. This was it. Enlightenment.

The bliss was like nothing I had known before. There was so much joy; yet at the same time it was all so peaceful. I meditated till very late, slept very little, and rose in time to begin more meditation in the monastery hall, well before the 3.00 a.m. bell. Usually at 3.00 a.m., in the hot and humid Thai forests, I would struggle with dullness and sleepiness. But not this morning. My body was effortlessly upright, mindfulness was as sharp as a scalpel, and concentration focused easily. It was so wonderful being enlightened. It was also so disappointing that it didn't last all that long.

In those days in northeast Thailand, the food was disgusting. For instance, once our single meal of the day consisted of just a ball of sticky rice with a medium-sized boiled frog on the top. There were no vegetables, no fruit, just frog-and-rice, and that was all for the day. I started by picking at the meat on the legs, and after at the frog's innards. A monk sitting close to me also started picking at the organs of the frog. Unfortunately, he pressed the frog's bladder. There was still urine inside. So the frog peed all over his rice. He stopped eating after that.

Usually, our main dish every day was rotten fish curry, and it was made of rotten fish. The small fish, caught during the rainy season, would be stored in earthen jars and used throughout the year. I found such a jar once, while cleaning around our monastery kitchen. It was full of crawling maggots so I went to throw it away. The headman of the village, the most educated and refined of them all, saw me and told me not to throw it away.

'But it's got maggots in it!' I protested.

'Even more delicious!' he replied, and took the jar from me.

The next day we had rotten fish curry for our one meal of the day.

The day after my enlightenment, I was surprised to see two saucepans of curry to flavour our sticky rice. One was the usual stinking rotten fish curry, the other an edible pork curry. Today, I thought, I will have a good meal for a change, to celebrate my attainment.

The abbot chose his food ahead of me. He took three huge ladlefuls of the delicious pork curry—the glutton. There was still plenty left for me. However, before passing the pot over to me, he began to pour my mouth-watering pork curry into the pot of rotten fish curry. Then he stirred it all together saying, 'It's all the same anyway.'

I was speechless. I was fuming. I was incensed. If he really thought it 'all the same anyway', then why did he take three whopping portions of pork curry for himself first, before mixing it together? The hypocrite! Moreover, he was a local boy who grew up with stinking rotten fish curry, and so should like it. The fake! The pig! The cheat!

Then a realisation hit me. Enlightened ones do not have preferences over food, nor do they get angry and call their abbots, albeit under the breath, pigs! I sure was angry and that meant—oh no!—that I wasn't enlightened after all.

The fire of my anger was immediately dampened by sodden depression. Thick dark clouds of dismay rolled in on my heart and completely obscured the sun that once was my enlightenment. Downcast and in gloom, I slopped two ladles of smelly rotten fish and pork curry onto my rice. I didn't care what I ate now; I was so dispirited. Finding out that I wasn't enlightened after all spoiled my whole day.

The road hog

On the subject of pigs, a wealthy specialist doctor had just purchased a very expensive and powerful new sports car. Of course, you don't spend so much money on a high-powered vehicle just to drive it in the slow city traffic. So one sunny day, he drove out of the city into the serene farming country. On reaching the speed camera free zone, he pressed hard on the accelerator and felt his sports car surge. With the engine roaring loudly and the sleek vehicle screaming along the country road, the doctor smiled with the exhilaration of high speed.

Not so exhilarated was a weather-worn farmer leaning on a paddock gate. Yelling at the top of his voice in order to be heard above the noise of the sports car, the farmer shouted, 'Pig!'

The doctor knew that he was acting wilfully, completely insensitive to the tranquillity of his surroundings, but he thought, 'What the hell! I have a right to enjoy myself.'

So he turned and yelled at the farmer, 'Who are you calling a pig?'

In those few seconds that he took his eyes off the road, his car ran into a pig in the middle of the road!

His brand new sports car was a total wreck. And as for the pig, he spent many weeks in a hospital bed and lost a great deal of money, as well as his car.

Hare Krishna

In the previous story, the doctor's ego had caused him to badly misjudge the warning of a kind-hearted farmer. In the following story, my monk's ego caused me to badly misjudge another kind-hearted person, much to my distress.

I was finishing a visit to my mother in London. She was walking alongside me to Ealing Broadway railway station to help with my ticket. On the way to the station, in busy Ealing High Street, I heard someone jeering, 'Hare Krishna! Hare Krishna!'

Being a bald-headed Buddhist monk wearing brown robes, I often get confused with the devotees of the Krishna-Consciousness movement. Many times in Australia, louts would try to ridicule me, usually from a safe distance, by shouting 'Hare Krishna! Hey! Hare Krishna!' and mocking my appearance. I quickly spotted the man shouting 'Hare Krishna!' and decided to be assertive by taking him to task for publicly abusing a good Buddhist monk.

With my mother just behind me, I said to the young man wearing jeans, jacket and a beanie, 'Look, friend! I'm a Buddhist monk, not a 'Hare Krishna' follower. You should know better. It's just not on that you shout 'Hare Krishna' at me!'

The young man smiled and took off his beanie, revealing a long pony-tail on the back of an otherwise bald head. 'Yeah, I know!' he said.'You're a Buddhist monk. I'm a Hare Krishna. Hare Krishna! Hare Krishna!'

He wasn't jeering at me after all, just doing his Hare Krishna thing. I was terribly embarrassed. Why do these things only happen when your mother is with you?

The hammer

We all make mistakes from time to time. Life is about learning to make our mistakes less often. To realise this goal, we have a policy in our monastery that monks are allowed to make mistakes. When the monks are not afraid to make mistakes, they don't make so many.

While walking through my monastery grounds one day, I found a hammer left out in the grass. It had obviously been there a long time, for it was already getting rusty. I was very disappointed at the carelessness of my fellow monks. All the things we use in our monastery, from our robes to the tools, are donated by our hard-working lay supporters. A poor but generous lay Buddhist might have saved up for weeks to buy that hammer for us. It just wasn't on to treat gifts so inconsiderately. So I called a meeting of the monks.

I am told that my character is usually as soft as mushy peas, but that evening I was as fierce as Thai chilli. I really gave my monks a tongue-lashing. They needed to be taught a lesson and learn to look after the few possessions we have. When I completed my harangue, all the monks were sitting bolt upright, ashen-faced and silent. I waited a while, expecting the culprit to confess, but none of the monks did. They all sat rigid, silent and waiting.

I felt very disillusioned with my fellow monks as I got up to go out of the hall. At the very least, I would have thought, the monk responsible for leaving the hammer out in the grass would have the guts to confess and apologise. Perhaps my talk had been too harsh?

As I walked out of the hall, I suddenly realised why none of the monks had admitted responsibility. I turned around and went back inside the hall.

'Monks,' I announced, 'I've found out who left that hammer out in the grass. It was me!'

I had clean forgotten that it was I who had been working outside and, in haste, had failed to put the hammer away. Even during my fiery talk, the memory had eluded me. Only after telling all my monks off did it all come back to me, in both senses of the meaning. It was I who had done it. Oooh! That was embarrassing!

Fortunately, we are all allowed to make mistakes in my monastery, even the abbot.

Enjoying a joke at no one's expense

When you abandon your ego, then no one can mock you. If someone calls you a fool, then the reason you get upset can only be that you believe they may be right!

When I was being driven along a multi-lane highway in Perth some years ago, some young men in an old car spotted me and began to jeer at me through their car's open window, 'Hey! Baldy! Oi! Skinhead!'

As they tried to wind me up, I wound my window down, and shouted back, 'Get your hair cut! Ya bunch of girls!' Perhaps I shouldn't have done that. It simply encouraged the young men.

The young larrikins steered their vehicle alongside mine, pulled out a magazine and, with mouths wide open, began gesticulating wildly to get me to look at the pictures in the magazine. It was a copy of *Playboy*.

I laughed at their irreverent sense of humour. I would have done the same when I was their age and out with my mates. After seeing me laugh, they soon drove off. Laughing at abuse was a better alternative than prudish embarrassment.

And did I look at the pictures in the *Playboy* magazine? Of course not, I'm a well-behaved celibate monk. So how did I know it was a copy of *Playboy*? Because my driver told me. At least, that's the story I'm sticking to.

The idiot

Someone calls you an idiot. Then you start thinking, 'How can they call me an idiot? They've got no right to call me an idiot! How rude to call me an idiot! I'll get them back for calling me an idiot.' And you suddenly realise that you have just let them call you an idiot another four times.

Every time you remember what they said, you allow them to call you an idiot. Therein lies the problem.

If someone calls you an idiot and you immediately let it go, then it doesn't bother you. There is the solution.

Why allow other people to control your inner happiness?

Suffering and letting go

Thinking about washing

People these days think too much. If they would only quieten their thinking process a little, then their lives would flow much easier.

One night each week in our monastery in Thailand, the monks would forgo their sleep to meditate all night in the main hall. It was part of our forest monk's tradition. It wasn't too austere since we could always take a nap the following morning.

One morning after the all-night meditation session, when we were about to go back to our huts to catch up on our sleep, the abbot beckoned a junior Australian-born monk. To the monk's dismay, the abbot gave him a huge pile of robes to wash, ordering him to do it immediately. It was our tradition to look after the abbot by washing his robes and doing other little services for him.

This was an enormous pile of washing. Moreover, all washing had to be done in the traditional way of the forest monks. Water had to be hauled from a well, a big fire made and the water boiled. A log from a jack fruit tree would be pared into chips with the monastery's machete. The chips would be added to the boiling water to release their sap, which would act as the 'detergent'. Then each robe would be placed singly in a long wooden trough, the brown boiling water poured over, and the robe would be pounded by hand until it was clean. The monk had then to dry the robes in the sun, turning them from time to time to ensure that the natural dye did not streak. To wash even one robe was a long and burdensome process. To wash such a large number of robes would take many hours. The young Brisbane-born monk was tired from not sleeping all night. I felt sorry for him.

I went over to the washing shed to give him a hand. When I got there, he was swearing and cursing more in Brisbane tradition than Buddhist tradition. He was complaining how unfair and cruel it was. 'Couldn't that abbot have waited until tomorrow? Didn't he realise that I haven't slept all night? I didn't become a monk for this!' That was not precisely what he said, but this is all that is printable.

When this occurred, I had been a monk for several years. I understood what he was experiencing and knew the way out of his problem. I told him, 'Thinking about it is much harder than doing it.'

He fell silent and stared at me. After a few moments of silence, he quietly went back to work and I went off for a sleep. Later that day, he came to see me to say thank you for helping with the washing. It was so true, he discovered, that thinking about it was the hardest part. When he stopped complaining and just did the washing, there was no problem at all.

The hardest part of anything in life is thinking about it.

A moving experience

I learned the priceless lesson that 'the hardest part of anything in life is thinking about it' in my early years as a monk in northeast Thailand. Ajahn Chah was constructing his monastery's new ceremonial hall and many of us monks were helping with the work. Ajahn Chah used to test us out by saying that a monk would work hard all day for just one or two Pepsis, which was much cheaper for the monastery than hiring labourers from town. Often I thought of starting a trade union for junior monks.

The ceremonial hall was constructed on a monk-made hill. There was much earth remaining from the mound. So Ajahn Chah called us monks together and told us that he wanted the remaining earth moved around to the back. For the next three days, working from 10.00 a.m. until well past dark, we shovelled and wheelbarrowed that great amount of earth to the very place that Ajahn Chah wanted. I was happy to see it finished.

The following day, Ajahn Chah left to visit another monastery for a few days. After he left, the deputy abbot called us monks together and told us that the earth was in the wrong place and had to be moved. I was annoyed, yet I managed to subdue my complaining mind as we all laboured hard for another three days in the tropical heat.

Just after we had finished moving the heap of earth for the second time, Ajahn Chah returned. He called us monks together and said, 'Why did you move the earth there? I told you it was to go in that other spot. Move it back there!'

I was angry. I was livid. I was ropeable. 'Can't those senior monks decide among themselves first? Buddhism is supposed to be an organised religion, but this monastery is so disorganised it can't even organise where to put some dirt! They can't do this to me!'

Three more long, tiring days loomed ahead of me. I was cursing in English, so the Thai monks wouldn't understand me, as I pushed the leaden wheelbarrows. This was beyond the pale. When would this stop?

I began to notice that the angrier I was, the heavier the wheelbarrow felt. One of my fellow monks saw me grumbling, came over and told me, 'Your trouble is that you think too much!'

He was so right. As soon as I stopped whingeing and whining, the wheelbarrow felt much lighter to push. I learned my lesson. Thinking about moving the earth was the hardest part; moving it was easy.

To this day, I suspect that Ajahn Chah and his deputy abbot planned it as it happened from the very start.

Poor me; lucky them

Life as a very junior monk in Thailand seemed so unfair. The senior monks received the best food, sat on the softest cushions and never had to push wheelbarrows. Whereas my one meal of the day was disgusting; I had to sit for long hours in ceremonies on the hard concrete floor (which was lumpy as well, because the villagers were hopeless at laying concrete); and sometimes I had to labour very hard. Poor me; lucky them.

I spent long, unpleasant hours justifying my complaints to myself. The senior monks were probably so enlightened that delicious food would be wasted on them, therefore I should get the best food. The senior monks had been sitting cross-legged on hard floors for years and were used to it, therefore I should get the big soft cushions. Moreover, the senior monks were all fat anyway, from eating the best food, so had 'natural upholstery' to their posteriors. The senior monks just told us junior monks to do the work, never labouring themselves, so how could they appreciate how hot and tiring pushing wheelbarrows was? The projects were all their ideas anyway, so they should do the work! Poor me; lucky them.

When I became a senior monk, I ate the best food, sat on a soft cushion and did little physical work. However, I caught myself envying the junior monks. They didn't have to give all the public talks, listen to people's problems all day and spend hours on administration. They had no responsibilities and so much time for themselves. I heard myself saying, 'Poor me; lucky them!'

I soon figured out what was going on. Junior monks have 'junior monk suffering'. Senior monks have 'senior monk suffering'. When I became a senior monk, I was just exchanging one form of suffering for another form of suffering.

It is precisely the same for single people who envy those who are married, and for married people who envy those who are single. As we all should know by now, when we get married, we are only exchanging 'single person's suffering' for 'married person's suffering'. Then when we get divorced, we are only exchanging 'married person's suffering' for 'single person's suffering'. Poor me; lucky them.

When we are poor, we envy those who are rich. However, many who are rich envy the sincere friendships and freedom from responsibilities of those who are poor. Becoming rich is only exchanging 'poor person's suffering' for 'rich person's suffering'. Retiring and taking a cut in your income is only exchanging 'rich person's suffering' for 'poor person's suffering'. And so it goes on. Poor me; lucky them.

To think that you will be happy by becoming something else is delusion. Becoming something else just exchanges one form of suffering for another form of suffering. But when you are content with who you are now, junior or senior, married or single, rich or poor, then you are free of suffering. Lucky me; poor them.

Advice for when you are sick

In my second year as a monk in northeast Thailand, I came down with scrub typhus. The fever was so strong that I was admitted to the monks' ward in the regional hospital at Ubon. In those days, in the mid-1970s, Ubon was a remote backwater of a very poor country. Feeling weak and afflicted, with a drip in my arm, I noticed the male nurse leave his station at 6.00 p.m. Half an hour later, the replacement nurse had yet to arrive, so I asked the monk in the next bed if we should alert someone in charge that the night nurse hadn't come. I was quickly told that in the monks' ward, there never is a night nurse. If you take a turn for the worse during the night, that's just unlucky karma. It was bad enough being very sick; now I was terrified as well!

For the next four weeks, every morning and afternoon a nurse built like a water buffalo would inject my buttocks with antibiotics. This was a poor public hospital in an undeveloped area of a third-world country, so the needles were recycled many more times than would be allowed even in Bangkok. That strong-armed nurse literally had to stab the needle with considerable force to enter the flesh. Monks were expected to be tough, but my buttocks weren't: they became very sore. I hated that nurse at that time.

I was in pain, I was weak, and I had never felt so miserable in my life. Then, one afternoon, Ajahn Chah came into the monks' ward to visit me. To visit me! I felt so flattered and impressed. I was uplifted. I felt great—until Ajahn Chah opened his mouth. What he said, I later found out, he told many sick monks whom he visited in hospital.

He told me, 'You'll either get better, or you'll die.'

Then he went away.

My elation was shattered. My joy at the visit vanished. The worst thing was that you couldn't fault Ajahn Chah. What he said was absolute truth. I'll get better or I'll die. Either way, the discomfort of the sickness will not last. Surprisingly, that was very reassuring. As it happened, I got better instead of dying. What a great teacher Ajahn Chah was.

What's wrong with being sick?

In my public talks, I often ask the audience to raise their hand if they have ever been sick. Nearly everyone puts up their hand. (Those who don't are either asleep or probably lost in a sexual fantasy!) This proves, I argue, that it is quite normal to be sick. In fact, it would be very unusual if you didn't fall sick from time to time. So why, I ask, do you say when you visit the doctor, 'There is something *wrong* with me, doctor'? It would be wrong only if you weren't sick sometimes. Thus a rational person should say instead, 'There is something *right* with me, doctor. I'm sick again!'

Whenever you perceive sickness as something *wrong*, you add unnecessary stress, even guilt, on top of the unpleasantness. In the nineteenth-century novel *Erehwon*, Samuel Butler envisaged a society in which illness was considered a crime and the sick were punished with a jail term. In one memorable passage, the accused man, sniffling and sneezing in the dock, was berated by the judge as a serial offender. This was not the first time he had appeared before the magistrate with a cold. Moreover, it was all his fault through eating junk food, failing to exercise adequately, and following a stressful lifestyle. He was sentenced to several years in jail.

How many of us are led to feel guilty when we are sick?

A fellow monk had been sick with an unknown illness for many years. He would spend day after day, week after week, in bed all day, too weak even to walk beyond his room. The monastery spared no expense or effort arranging every kind of medical therapy, orthodox and alternative, in an attempt to help him, but nothing seemed to work. He would think he was feeling better, stagger outside for a little walk, and then relapse for weeks. Many times they thought he would die.

One day, the wise abbot of the monastery had an insight into the problem. So he went to the sick monk's room. The bedridden monk stared up at the abbot with utter hopelessness.

'I've come here,' said the abbot, 'on behalf of all the monks and nuns of this monastery, and also for all the laypeople who support us. On behalf of all these people who love and care for you, I have come to give you permission to die. You don't have to get better.'

At those words, the sick monk wept. He'd been trying so hard to get better. His friends had gone to so much trouble trying to help heal his sick body that he couldn't bear to disappoint them. He felt such a failure, so guilty, for not getting better. On hearing the abbot's words, he now felt free to be sick, even to die. He didn't need to struggle so hard to please his friends anymore. The release he felt caused him to cry.

What do you think happened next? From that day on, he began to recover.

Visiting the sick

How many of us say, 'How are you feeling today?' when visiting a loved one in hospital?

For a start, what a stupid thing to say! Of course they're feeling rotten, otherwise they wouldn't be in hospital, would they? Furthermore, the common greeting puts the patient in profound psychological stress. They feel it would be an act of rudeness to upset their visitors by telling the truth that they feel terrible. How can they disappoint someone who has taken the time and trouble to come and visit them in hospital by honestly replying that they feel awful, as drained as a used tea bag? So instead, they may feel compelled to lie, saying, 'I think I feel a little better today', meanwhile feeling guilty that they aren't doing enough to get better. Unfortunately, too many hospital visitors make the patients feel more ill!

An Australian nun of the Tibetan Buddhist tradition was dying of cancer in a hospice in Perth. I had known her for several years and would visit her often. One day she phoned me at my monastery, requesting I visit her that very day as she felt her time was close. So I dropped what I was doing and immediately got someone to drive me the seventy kilometres to the hospice in Perth. When I checked in at the hospice reception, an authoritarian nurse told me that the Tibetan Buddhist nun had given strict instructions that no one was to visit her.

'But I have come from so far especially to see her,' I gently said.

'I'm sorry,' barked the nurse, 'she does not want any visitors and we all must respect that.'

'But that cannot be so,' I protested. 'She phoned me only an hour and a half ago and asked me to come.'

The senior nurse glared at me and ordered me to follow her. We stopped in front of the Aussie nun's room where the nurse pointed to the big paper sign taped to the closed door.

'ABSOLUTELY NO VISITORS!'

'See!' said the nurse.

As I examined the notice, I read some more words, written in smaller letters underneath: '... except Ajahn Brahm.'

So I went in.

When I asked the nun why she had put up the notice with the special exception, she explained that when all her other friends and relations came to visit her, they became so sad and miserable seeing her dying that it made her feel much worse. 'It's bad enough dying from cancer', she said, 'but it's too much to deal with my visitors' emotional problems as well.'

She went on to say that I was the only friend who treated her as a person, not as someone dying; who didn't get upset at seeing her gaunt and wasted, but instead told her jokes and made her laugh. So I told her jokes for the next hour, while she taught me how to help a friend with their death. I learnt from her that when you visit someone in hospital, talk to the person and leave the doctors and nurses to talk to the sickness.

She died less than two days after my visit.

The lighter side of death

As a Buddhist monk, I often have to deal with death. It is part of my job to conduct Buddhist funeral services. As a result, I know many of the funeral directors in Perth on a personal basis. Perhaps it is because of the requirement for public solemnity that in private they show a great sense of humour.

For instance, one funeral director told me of a cemetery in South Australia located in a clay-based hollow. They had seen it happen several times, they told me, that just after they had lowered the coffin into the grave, a heavy shower would come and water would pour into the hole. With the priest saying the prayers, the coffin would slowly float up into full view!

Then there was the vicar in Perth who, at the very beginning of the service, inadvertently leant on all of the buttons on the lectern. All at once, and in the middle of his reading, the coffin began moving through the curtain, his microphone cut out, and the bugle calls of The Last Post reverberated through the chapel! It didn't help that the deceased was a pacifist.

One particular funeral director was of the habit of telling me jokes as we walked together ahead of the hearse, and the following cortege, through the cemetery to the grave side. At the punch line to each of his jokes, which were all very funny, he would dig me in the ribs with his elbow and try to make me laugh. It was all I could do to resist laughing out loud. So, as we approached the place for the service I had to tell him very firmly to stop misbehaving so I could arrange my face in a countenance more befitting to the occasion. That only incited him to begin another joke, the swine!

Over the years, though, I have learned to lighten up at my Buddhist funerals. A few years ago, I summoned up the courage to tell a joke for the first time at a funeral service. Shortly after I began the joke, the funeral director, standing at the back of the bereaved, figured out what I was about to do and made faces at me, desperately trying to make me stop. It is simply not done to crack a joke at a funeral service. But I was determined. The funeral director's face went whiter than one of his corpses. At the end of the joke, the mourners in the chapel broke freely into laughter, and the funeral director's once-contorted face relaxed with relief. The family and friends all congratulated me afterwards. They said how much the deceased would have enjoyed that particular joke and how he would have been pleased that his loved ones had sent him off with a smile. I often tell that joke at funeral services now. Why not? Would you like your relations and friends to hear me tell a joke at your funeral service? Every time I have asked that question, the answer is always 'Yes!'

So what was that joke?

An elderly couple had been together so long that when one passed away, the other died only a few days later. Thus they appeared in heaven together. A beautiful angel took them both to an impressive mansion on top of a cliff overlooking the ocean. In this life, only billionaires could afford such outstanding real estate. The angel announced that the mansion was theirs as their heavenly reward.

The husband had been a practical man and immediately said, 'That's all very well, but I don't think we could afford the annual council rates on such a big property.'

The angel smiled sweetly and told them that there were no government taxes on property in heaven. Then he took the couple on a tour of the many rooms in the mansion. Each room was furnished in exquisite taste, some with antique furniture, some with modern. Priceless chandeliers dripped from many ceilings. Taps of solid gold gleamed in every bathroom. There were DVD systems and state-of-the-art widescreen televisions. At the end of the tour, the angel said that if there was anything they didn't like, just let him know and he would change it at once. This was their heavenly reward.

The husband had been reckoning the value of all the contents and said, 'These are very expensive furnishings. I don't think we could afford the property insurance premium.'

The angel rolled his eyes and told them gently that thieves weren't allowed to enter heaven, so there wasn't any need for property insurance. Then he led them both downstairs to the mansion's triple-spaced garage. There was a huge, new SUV four-wheel drive next to a glittering Rolls- Royce Touring limousine, and the third car was a limited edition red Ferrari sports car with retractable roof. The husband had always wanted a powerful sports car in his earthly life, but could only dream of ever owning one. The angel said that if they wished to change the models, or the colours, they should not hesitate to let him know. This was their heavenly reward.

The husband glumly said, 'Even if we could afford the vehicle registration fees, which we can't, what's the point of a fast sports car these days? I'll only end up getting fined for speeding.'

The angel shook his head and told them patiently that there were no vehicle registration fees up in heaven, nor were there any speed cameras. He could drive the Ferrari as fast as he liked. Then the angel opened the garage doors. On the opposite side of the road was a magnificent eighteen-hole golf course. The angel said that they knew up in heaven how much the husband liked his golf, adding that this wonderful golf course had been designed by Tiger Woods himself.

Still the husband looked unhappy as he said, 'That is an expensive looking golf club, judging by the clubhouse, and I don't think I could afford the club fees.'

The angel groaned, then recovering his saintly composure reassured the husband that *there are no fees in heaven*. Moreover, in golf courses in heaven you never have to queue to tee off, the ball always misses the bunkers, and the greens are so designed that whichever way you putt the ball, it will always curl into the hole. This was their heavenly reward.

After the angel left them, the husband began to scold his wife. He was so angry with her that he yelled and ranted and reprimanded her something terrible. She couldn't understand why he was so angry.

'Why are you so upset at me?' she pleaded, 'We have this wonderful mansion and lovely furniture. You've got your Ferrari, which you may drive as fast as you want, and a golf course just across the road. Why are you so angry at me?'

'Because, wife,' the husband said bitterly, 'if it wasn't for all that health food you gave me, I could have been up here years ago!'

Grief, loss and celebrating a life

Grief is what we add on to loss. It is a learned response, specific to some cultures only. It is not unavoidable.

I found this out through my own experience of being immersed for over eight years in a pure, Asian-Buddhist culture. In those early years in a Buddhist forest monastery in a remote corner of Thailand, Western culture and ideas were totally unknown. My monastery served as the local cremation ground for many surrounding villages. There was a cremation almost weekly. In the hundreds of funerals I witnessed there in the late 1970s, never once did I see anyone cry. I would speak with the bereaved family in the following days and still there were no signs of grief. One had to conclude that there was no grief. I came to know that in northeast Thailand in those days, a region steeped in Buddhist teachings for many centuries, death was accepted by all in a way that defied Western theories of grief and loss.

Those years taught me that there is an alternative to grief. Not that grief is wrong, only that there is another possibility. Loss of a loved one can be viewed in a second way, a way that avoids the long days of aching grief.

My own father died when I was only sixteen. He was, for me, a great man. He was the one who helped me find the meaning of love with his words, 'Whatever you do in your life, Son, the door of my heart will always be open to you.' Even though my love for him was huge, I never cried at his funeral service. Nor have I cried for him since. I have never felt like crying over his premature death. It took me many years to understand my emotions surrounding his death. I found that understanding through the following story, which I share with you here.

As a young man I enjoyed music, all types of music from rock to classical, jazz to folk. London was a fabulous city in which to grow up in the 1960s and early 1970s, especially when you loved music. I remember being at the very first nervous performance of the band Led Zeppelin at a small club in Soho. On another occasion, only a handful of us watched the then unknown Rod Stewart front a rock group in the upstairs room of a small pub in North London. I have so many precious memories of the music scene in London at that time.

At the end of most concerts I would shout 'More! More!' along with many others. Usually, the band or orchestra would play on for a while. Eventually, though, they had to stop, pack up their gear and go home. And so did I. It seems to my memory that every evening when I walked home from the club, pub or concert hall, it was always raining. There is a special word to describe the dreary type of rain often met with in London: drizzle. It always seemed to be drizzling, cold and gloomy as I left the concert halls. But even though I knew in my heart that I probably would never get to hear that band again, that they had left my life forever, never once did I feel sad or cry. As I walked out into the cold, damp darkness of the London night, the stirring music still echoed in my mind, 'What magnificent music! What a powerful performance! How lucky I was to have been there at the time!' I never felt grief at the end of a great concert.

That is exactly how I felt after my own father's death. It was as if a great concert had finally come to an end. It was such a wonderful performance. I was, as it were, shouting loudly 'More! More!' when it came close to the finale. My dear old dad did struggle hard to keep living a little longer for us. But the moment eventually came when he had to 'pack up his gear and go home'. When I walked out of the crematorium at Mortlake at the end of the service into the cold London drizzle—I remember the drizzle clearly—knowing in my heart that I would probably not get to be with him again, that he had left my life forever, I didn't feel sad; nor did I cry. What I felt in my heart was, 'What a magnificent father! What a powerful inspiration was his life. How lucky I was to have been there at the time. How fortunate I was to have been his son.' As I held my mother's hand on the long walk into the future, I felt the very same exhilaration as I had often felt at the end of one of the great concerts in my life. I wouldn't have missed that for the world. Thank you, Dad.

Grief is seeing only what has been taken away from you. The celebration of a life is recognising all that we were blessed with, and feeling so very grateful.

Falling leaves

Probably the hardest of deaths for us to accept is that of a child. On many occasions I have had the honour to conduct the funeral service for a small boy or girl, someone not long set out on their experience of life. My task is to help lead the distraught parents, and others as well, beyond the torment of guilt and through the obsessive demand for an answer to the question, 'Why?'

I often relate the following parable, which was told to me in Thailand many years ago.

A simple forest monk was meditating alone in the jungle in a hut made of thatch. Late one evening, there was a very violent monsoon storm. The wind roared like jet aircraft and heavy rain thrashed against his hut. As the night grew denser, the storm grew more savage. First, branches could be heard being ripped off the trees. Then whole trees were uprooted by the force of the gale and came crashing to the ground with a sound as loud as the thunder.

The monk soon realised that his grass hut was no protection. If a tree fell on top of his hut, or even a big branch, it would break clean through the grass roof and crush him to death. He didn't sleep the whole night. Often during that night, he would hear huge forest giants smash their way to the ground and his heart would pound for a while.

In the hours before dawn, as so often happens, the storm disappeared. At first light, the monk ventured outside his grass hut to inspect the damage. Many big branches, as well as two sizeable trees, had just missed his hut. He felt lucky to have survived. What suddenly took his attention, though, was not the many uprooted trees and fallen branches scattered on the ground, but the many leaves that now lay spread thickly on the forest floor.

As he expected, most of the leaves lying dead on the ground were old brown leaves, which had lived a full life. Among the brown leaves were many yellow leaves. There were even several green leaves. And some of those green leaves were of such a fresh and rich green colour that he knew they could have only unfurled from the bud a few hours before. In that moment, the monk's heart understood the nature of death.

He wanted to test the truth of his insight so he gazed up to the branches of the trees. Sure enough, most of the leaves still left on the trees were young healthy green ones, in the prime of their life. Yet, although many newborn green leaves lay dead on the ground, old bent and curled up brown leaves still clung on to the branches. The monk smiled; from that day on, the death of a child would never disconcert him.

When the storms of death blow through our families, they usually take the old ones, the 'mottled brown leaves'. They also take many middle-aged ones, like the yellow leaves of a tree. Young people die too, in the prime of their life, similar to the green leaves. And sometimes death rips from dear life a small number of young children, just as nature's storms rip off a small number of young shoots. This is the essential nature of death in our communities, as it is the essential nature of storms in a forest.

There is no one to blame and no one to lay guilt on for the death of a child. This is the nature of things. Who can blame the storm? And it helps us to answer the question of why some children die. The answer is the very same reason why a small number of young green leaves must fall in a storm.

The ups and downs of death

Perhaps the most emotional moment of the funeral service is the time when the coffin is lowered into the grave or, in a cremation, when the button is pressed to move the casket. It is as if the last physical reminder of a loved one is finally being stolen from the bereaved forever. It is often the moment when tears can no longer be held back.

Such moments are particularly difficult in some crematoriums in Perth. There, when the button is pressed, the casket descends into a basement complex where the ovens are located. It is meant to replicate a burial. However, a dead person going down has the subconscious symbolism of going down to hell! It is already bad enough losing their loved one; adding the intimation of descent to the underworld is often too hard to bear.

Therefore, I once proposed that crematorium chapels be constructed so that when the priest pressed the button to commit the deceased, the coffin would rise up gracefully into the air. A simple hydraulic lift would easily suffice. As the casket approached the ceiling it could disappear in swirling clouds of dry ice, and through a trapdoor into the roof cavity above, all to the sound of sweet heavenly music. What a wonderful psychological uplift that would give to the mourners!

However, some who have learnt of my proposal have advised that it might take away from the integrity of the ceremony, especially in such cases where everyone knows that the dead scoundrel in the coffin would hardly go 'up there'. So I refined my proposal, suggesting that there could be three buttons for committal to cover all cases: an 'up' button only for the goodly, a 'down' button to take care of the rascals, and a 'sideways' button for the ambiguous majority. Then, in recognition of the democratic principles of Western society, and to further add interest to an otherwise dreary rite, I could ask for a show of hands from the mourners to vote on which of the three buttons to press! This would make funeral services most memorable occasions, with a very good reason for going.

The man with four wives

A man, who was successful in life, maintained four wives. When his life was about to end, he called to his bedside his fourth wife, the most recent and youngest.

'Darling,' he said, stroking her legendary figure, 'in a day or two I will be dead. After death, I will be lonely without you. Will you come with me?'

'No way!' declared the illustrious girl. 'I must stay behind. I will speak your praises at your funeral, but I can do no more.' And she strode out of his bedroom.

Her cold refusal was like a dagger to his heart. He had given so much attention to his youngest wife. He was so proud of her in fact that he chose her as his escort to important functions. She gave him dignity in his old age. It was a surprise to find out that she did not love him as he had loved her.

Still, he had three more wives, so he called in the third wife he had married in middle-age. He had worked so hard to win the hand of his third wife. He loved her deeply for making so many joys possible for him. She was so attractive that many men desired her; yet she had always been faithful. She gave him a sense of security.

'Sweetheart,' he said, grasping her tightly, 'in a day or two I will be dead. After death, I will be lonely without you. Will you come with me?'

'Absolutely not!' asserted the seductive young woman in a businesslike manner. 'Such a thing has never been done. I will give you a lavish funeral, but after the service I will go with your sons.'

His third wife's future infidelity shook him to the core. He sent her away and called for his second wife.

He had grown up with his second wife. She wasn't so attractive but she was always there for him, to help him with any problems and give invaluable advice. She was his most trusted friend.

'Beloved,' he said, gazing into her confident eyes, 'in a day or two I will be dead. After death, I will be lonely without you. Will you come with me?'

'I'm sorry,' she said apologetically, 'I cannot go with you. I will go as far as your grave side, but no further.'

The old man was devastated. He called for his first wife, whom he had known seemingly forever. He had neglected her in recent years, especially after he had met his alluring third wife and distinguished fourth wife. But it was this first wife who was really important to him, working quietly behind the scenes. He felt ashamed when he saw her come in ill-dressed and very thin.

'Dearest,' he said imploringly, 'in a day or two I will be dead. After death, I will be lonely without you. Will you come with me?'

'Of course I'll go with you,' she replied impassively. 'I always go with you from life to life.'

The first wife was called Karma. The second wife's name was Family. The third wife was Wealth. And the fourth wife was Fame.

Please read the story once more, now that you know the four wives. Which of the wives is most important to take care of? Which will go with you when you die?

Cracking up

In my first year in Thailand, we would be taken from monastery to monastery in the back of a small truck. The senior monks had the best seats, of course, in the cab up front. We junior monks sat squashed on hard wooden benches on the rear tray. Above the benches was a low metal frame, over which was stretched a tarpaulin to protect us from rain and dust.

The roads were all dirt roads, poorly maintained. When the wheels met a pothole, the truck went down and the junior monks went up. Crack! Many times I cracked my head on those hard metal frames. Moreover, being a bald-headed monk, I had no 'padding' to cushion the blow.

I swore every time I hit my head—in English, of course, so the Thai monks couldn't understand. But when the Thai monks hit their heads, they only laughed! I couldn't figure it out. How can you laugh when you hit your head so painfully hard? Perhaps, I considered, those Thai monks had already hit their heads too many times and there had been some permanent damage.

Because I used to be a scientist, I decided to do an experiment. I resolved to laugh, like the Thai monks, the next time I cracked my head, just to see what it was like. You know what I discovered? I found out that if you laugh when you hit your head, it hurts much less.

Laughter releases endorphins into your bloodstream, which are nature's painkillers. It also enhances your immune system to fight off any infections. So it helps to laugh when you feel pain. If you still don't believe me, then try it the next time you hit your head.

The experience taught me that when life is painful, it hurts less when you see the funny side and manage a laugh.

The worm and his lovely pile of dung

Some people simply don't want to be free from trouble. If they haven't got enough problems of their own to worry about, then they tune in to the television soapies to worry about fictional characters' problems. Many take anxiety to be stimulating; they regard what is suffering to be good fun. They don't want to be happy, because they are too attached to their burdens.

Two monks had been close friends all their life. After they died, one was reborn a *deva* (a heavenly being) in a beautiful heaven world, while his friend was reborn as a worm in a pile of dung.

The deva soon began to miss his old friend and wondered where he'd been reborn. He couldn't find his friend anywhere in his own heaven world, so he looked in all the other heaven realms too. His friend wasn't there. Using his heavenly powers, the deva searched the world of human beings but couldn't find his friend there either. Surely, he thought, his friend wouldn't have taken rebirth in the animal realm, but he checked there just in case. Still there was no sign of his friend from the previous life. So, next, the deva searched the world of what we call the 'creepy-crawlies' and, to his great surprise, there he found his friend reborn as a worm in a disgusting pile of stinking dung!

The bonds of friendship are so strong that they often outlast death. The deva felt he had to rescue his old companion from such an unfortunate rebirth, no matter what karma had led to it.

So the deva appeared in front of the foul pile of dung and called out, 'Hey, worm! Do you remember me? We were monks together in our past life and you were my best friend. Whereas I've been reborn in a most delightful heaven world, you've been reborn in this revolting pile of cow-shit. Don't be worried, though, because I can take you to heaven with me. Come on, old friend!'

'Hang on a moment!' said the worm, 'What's so great about this "heaven world" you are twittering on about? I'm very happy here with my fragrant, delicious pile of delectable dung, thank you very much.'

'You don't understand,' said the deva, and he gave the worm a brilliant description of the delights and pleasures of heaven.

'Is there any dung up there, then?' asked the worm, getting to the point.

'Of course not!' sniffed the deva.

'Then I ain't going!' replied the worm firmly. 'Nick off!' And the worm burrowed into the centre of the dung pile.

The deva thought that if only the worm could see heaven for himself, then he would understand. So the deva held his nose and thrust his soft hand into the repulsive pile of dung, searching for the worm. He found him and began to pull him out.

'Hey! Leave me alone!' screamed the worm. 'Help! May Day! I'm being worm-napped!' And the little slippery worm wriggled and squirmed till he got free, then he dived back into the dung pile to hide.

The kind deva plunged his fingers into the stinking faeces again, found the worm and tried once more to pull him out. The deva almost got the worm out, but because the worm was smeared with slimy filth and did not want to go he escaped a second time and hid even deeper in the dung pile. One hundred and eight times the deva tried to lead the poor worm out from his miserable dung pile, but the worm was so attached to his lovely pile of dung that he always wriggled back!

So, eventually, the deva had to go back up to heaven and leave the foolish worm to his 'lovely pile of dung'.

Thus end the hundred and eight stories told in this book.

Glossary

abbot Buddhist monasteries of our tradition have an abbot whose role combines that of teacher and administrator. Unlike many Christian monastic orders there is no rule of obedience to an abbot, although often the wishes of the abbot prevail.

Ajahn Chah Ajahn Chah was Ajahn Brahm's teacher from January 1975 until May 1983 when Ajahn Brahm arrived in Australia. Shortly after that, Ajahn Chah became very ill and was paralysed and unable to speak. He finally passed away on 16 January 1992, with the reputation of being one of the great enlightened masters of our time.

alms, begging for Monks of our tradition walk to the village for their food in the early morning. The villagers expect the monks and delight in giving them their daily meal by placing it silently in the monks' almsbowls. No words are exchanged in this moving act of creating good karma.

Buddha, the The name given to Sidhattha Gotama after his enlightenment under the bodhi tree in 588 BCE, and thus he is recognised as the founder of what is now called 'Buddhism'.

Buddhist A follower of the religion established by the Buddha, usually recognised by their virtuous conduct, harmlessness to all beings, compassion, and devotion to meditation.

Buddhist monastery A centre where many monks or nuns live, train and practise their duties.

Buddhist temple A religious building usually housing an image of the Buddha. It doesn't always have monks and nuns in residence.

deva This Sanskrit word literally means 'a shining being', and refers to a heavenly being, an angel, one who has been reborn into one of the several heavenly realms as a result of their good karma.

Jātaka stories These stories are part of the ancient scriptures of Buddhism which consist of fables with an edifying moral. Some stories are said to tell of the past lives of the Buddha.

karma, the law of The law of moral cause and effect, stating that the actions of body, speech and mind that bring happiness to others will bring happiness to oneself, but whatever causes harm to another will bring unhappiness to oneself.

lay Buddhists Buddhists, other than monks and nuns, who are the vast majority of the followers of the Buddha.

meditation The practice of 'letting go' to reach profound states of inner peace, freedom and bliss.

Middle Way The path to enlightenment travelled by the Buddha and then taught by him to the world. It avoids the two extremes of self-torment and sensual indulgence.

monk An ordained person keeping the rules of celibacy and simplicity. When monks first join the monastery they are ordained as a novice (meaning 'no vice'!) and they must keep less rules than the senior monks. When the monks take higher ordination, they undertake the full set of rules. A junior monk has spent less than five years as a monk, whereas a senior monk has more than ten years standing.

Rains Retreat (Vassa) The three-month period between the full moon of July and October when the monks and nuns stop all travel and devote themselves to intensive meditation and study.

Sutta A discourse by the Buddha.

Thai forest tradition A tradition of simplicity and devotion to meditation which has as one of its founding fathers Venerable Ajahn Mun of northeast Thailand. The followers of this tradition are known for their strict adherence to their precepts and deep skill in meditation practice.

Theravada One of the main schools of Buddhism said to be the closest, though not identical, to the original teachings of the Buddha. The school is dominant in Sri Lanka, Thailand, Burma, Cambodia and Laos. Theravadan Buddhism is now spreading rapidly in the West.

Wat Nong Pah Pong An important Thai monastery founded by Ajahn Chah, the name of which literally means 'the monastery of the forest thicket by the pond'.

Notes

Nearly all of the stories in this book have been handed down orally in our monastic tradition. Many have their roots in the ancient scriptures of Buddhism and are freely allowed to grow in each telling, so as to adapt to the times. However, a few other stories are more modern anecdotes that add to the richness of our Buddhist storytelling.

When the stories have evolved from a specific Buddhist text, the source is quoted below. Others have an untraceable source, probably being a story that I heard and remembered in the early part of my thirty-five years as a Buddhist. Some have since been retold in books and those re-tellings are acknowledged wherever possible. However, the main source of my material is my own life, especially my thirty years as a monk when these stories occurred, or were heard in the inspiring sermons in our monastic halls.

1 Devaputta Saṃyutta, Sutta No. 26, my own translation.

2 This story has evolved from a combination of other sources, in particular the origin story to Dhammapada, verse 110 and the verses of the enlightened monk Adhimutta Thera in the Theragāthā.

3 This story is rooted in Saṃyutta Nikāya, Kosala Saṃyutta, Sutta No. 8 and also in the Udāna, vagga 5, Sutta No. 1.

4 This story evolved from Saṃyutta Nikāya, Sakka Saṃyutta, Sutta No. 22.

5 I first heard a version of this ancient story as a young Buddhist in the United Kingdom. It has since been retold and published in brief by Indries Shah in *The Way of the Sufi*, Penguin Books, Harmondsworth, 1975, p. 80–1.

6 Permission to reproduce this previously unpublished poem 'It's Too Much to Hope For' by Jonathan Wilson-Fuller has been granted by the author.

7 According to my research, the story of the 'Three Questions' was first published in Yiddish in 1903 in a book that included short stories from other distinguished authors, such as Chekov, to aid the Jews who were being persecuted in Russia. The version that I read as a student at Cambridge University in 1970 was published in an anthology, although I cannot trace that publication.

8 This story is based on the Jātaka story No. 107.

9 This story is based on Jātaka story No. 215.

10 This story is based on Udāna, chapter 6, Sutta No. 4.

Of Related Interest from the BPS

Curbing Anger, Spreading Love
Bhikkhu Visuddhacāra

In an easy, conversational style, the author discusses sixteen ways to control and overcome anger, and offers instructions on how to practice the meditation on universal love.

BP 513S 112pp.

A Treasury of Buddhist Stories from the Dhammapada Commentary
E.W. Burlingame

A collection of fifty-six of the most popular and beloved Buddhist stories of all time, from Burlingame's classic translation of the background stories to the Dhammapada Commentary. Suitable for adults and young readers of age fourteen and over.

BP 220SA 250pp.

Great Disciples of the Buddha
Nyanaponika Thera & Hellmuth Hecker

This volume combines all past issues of the BPS's popular Lives of the Disciples series of Wheels. It offers inspiring and informative accounts of such great disciples of the Master as Ven. Sāriputta, Moggallāna, Ānanda, Mahā Kassapa, etc.

BP 417H 448pp.

Of related interest from the BPS

A Taste of Freedom
Ajahn Chah

This booklet contains 10 talks given by the renown Thai meditation master Venerable Ajahn Chah.
In his clear and simple, yet penetrative and profound style Ajahn Chah describes how one can realize true freedom and peace through the development of one's mind.

BP 525S 106pp.

The Four Sublime States & The Practice of Loving Kindness (Metta)
Nyanaponika Thera / Ñāṇamoli Thera

A combined issue of two Wheel classics.

BP 225S 64pp.

Technique of Living
Leonard A. Bullen

Drawing upon the Buddha's teachings on right mindfulness, the author has devised a practical program of self-training that deals with such problems as self-acceptance, the control of anxiety and resentment, the inferiority complex, detachment, etc.

BP 416S 142pp.

The Buddhist Publication Society

The BPS is an approved charity dedicated to making known the Teaching of the Buddha, which has a vital message for all people.

Founded in 1958, the BPS has published a wide variety of books and booklets covering a great range of topics. Its publications include accurate annotated translations of the Buddha's discourses, standard reference works, as well as original contemporary expositions of Buddhist thought and practice. These works present Buddhism as it truly is—a dynamic force which has influenced receptive minds for the past 2500 years and is still as relevant today as it was when it first arose.

For more information about the BPS and our publications, please visit our website or write an e-mail or letter to:

The Administrative Secretary
Buddhist Publication Society
P.O. Box 61
54, Sangharaja Mawatha
Kandy • Sri Lanka

Tel: 0094 81 223 7283 • Fax: 0094 81 222 3679
E-mail: bps@sltnet.lk
web site: http://www.bps.lk